PRAISE FOR
EQUIP YOUR INNER COACH

"After progressing from secretarial work to the role of vice president, Janet Bickel went on to start a successful business. This leader of prodigious energy has now shaped all she's learned from her fifty years of professional service into a gold mine of a book that is both edgy and well-documented, both gentle and incisive. The amount of useful wisdom that Janet has packed into these pages will amaze you."

—*Sharon Griswold, MD, Emergency Medicine Specialist*

"Discovering 'what you want to be when you grow up' turns out to be a lifelong, often lonely journey with more questions than answers. This book is the perfect combination of a handbook for the journey and a companion that facilitates reaping the benefits of your experiences along the way. What also sets it apart from other resources I've encountered is that it emphasizes reflection and situational awareness as key ingredients to finding fulfillment. Each section empowers professionals at all levels to understand the challenges and opportunities in their environment in new ways, such that their decisions are more purposeful and effective."

—*Alexandra Suchman, CEO, Barometer XP*

"Here is a power-packed book designed as a support for anyone struggling to be successful as well as healthy and fully human. Janet's enthusiasm around how to build all these skills shines from every chapter, rendering accessible a broad range of thorny subjects."

—*Kate Malliarakis, BSN, PhD, Associate Professor, Emerita, George Washington University School of Nursing, and President, KAM Associates*

"*Equip Your Inner Coach* teaches how befriending ourselves underlies every other professional development skill, including navigating complex organizations. This book is essential reading for professionals seeking to build a sustainable career of meaning and purpose and will be a boon to leaders at all levels. It will be required reading in the leadership courses I teach."

—*Niki Steckler, PhD, Professor of Management, Oregon Health & Sciences University*

"All of the breadth and depth of Janet's knowledge of career-building and leadership are evident in this well-structured and smartly designed book. Moreover, her focus on the extra challenges that women face will equip women to achieve more than they could have without this resource—at the same time as it also educates men to be more effective mentors and leaders."

—*Joshua T. Hanson MD, Associate Dean and Associate Professor of Medicine, Long School of Medicine, UT Health San Antonio*

"Janet has been a thought leader for decades on all the skills central to turning intellectual capital into career capital. Her deep thinking inspires the introspection necessary for self-realization and the communication skills key to community-building."

—*Kimberly A. Skarupski, PhD, Senior Associate Dean for Faculty Development, Johns Hopkins University School of Medicine*

"Janet Bickel engages readers in navigating the dimly lit stairway of advancement in a way that merges enhanced self-awareness with the skilled management of their complex work worlds. Translating her years of experience as an educator and coach, she has designed a resource useful not only to early- and mid-career professionals but also to emerging leaders and their mentors and coaches. The lessons are designed for everyone but will speak most directly to those who are marginalized by academic and organizational cultures in North America."

—Diane Magrane MD, Academic Leadership Development
Consultant, and Emerita Director, ELAM

"Readers of *Equip Your Inner Coach* will benefit from Janet Bickel's extensive and well-conveyed essence of what matters in leadership. This book will impact established leaders as well as many with high potential to guide us into the future. This book also does an exceptional job of reminding us of the challenges still confronting women aspiring to leadership roles."

—Frank Rosinia, MD MHCM ACC, Professor and Chair, Department of
Anesthesiology, Long School of Medicine, UT Health San Antonio

"This book will be of immediate value to many current and budding leaders, especially the chapters on handling conflicts and working with organizational complexities. I will be recommending it widely to junior colleagues as well."

—Annette J. Johnson, MD, Chair of Radiology,
Medical College of Georgia, Augusta University

EQUIP YOUR INNER COACH

Personal, Career, and Leadership Development in an Uncertain Age

JANET W. BICKEL

You only live once, but if you do it right, once is enough.

—Mae West

CONTENTS

INTRODUCTION

Do you want to increase your autonomy, competence and connections? Are you ready to address whatever might be interfering with your building and tapping into your own wisdom? This book offers guidance in identifying and understanding your strengths, weaknesses, emotions, motivations, and assumptions with greater clarity and friendliness. As self-efficacy expands, so does your agility in handling competition, conflicts, negotiations, organizational politics and transitions. You approach sensitive conversations and bridge differences with greater ease, leading to more authentic connections with others, our truest wealth. In these ways you enable and equip your own inner coach.

This career development resource for early and mid-career professionals is unique in three ways:

First, I work from the premise that softening toward ourselves is often what is hardest. This softening begins with facing our personal museum of embarrassments with curiosity and compassion. Treating self-doubts and insecurities as teachers rather than as failures speeds release from our finger-wagging inner critics.

Second, this book covers all the skills foundational to career-building and to growing as a leader in any field. Part 1 covers the inner work of building on your strengths, obtaining the feedback necessary to close gaps between your intentions and your actual impact, arriving at a definition of success based on your values, maintaining equanimity even when you feel devalued, and increasing your objectivity. Part 2 discusses the additional skills that working interdependently requires, including communicating across multiple kinds of differences, approaching

1

conflicts as learning opportunities, and navigating organizational politics. Part 3 focuses on the long haul, on building resilience, agility, and hopefully also a sense of humor about yourself as you mature.

While the chapters may be read in any order, I discuss the skills in the order in which they most logically build upon each other.

Third, threaded throughout this book are examples of how women can meet the challenges they still face in turning their intellectual capital into career capital. Career development can be compared to a poorly lit stairway with uneven steps and only sporadic handrails. Elevators are reserved for those with a powerful sponsor. With less access to handrails and elevators, women and people of color generally do not climb as high as white-skinned men. Women and people of color remain hampered by invisible weights of cultural and systemic restrictions which many have internalized. Paleontologist Stephen Jay Gould observed: "Few tragedies can be more extensive than the stunting of life, few injustices deeper than the denial of an opportunity to strive or even to hope, by a limit imposed from without, but falsely identified as lying within."[1] When women look around and see mainly women on the lower stairs while men are steadily climbing, too many convince themselves that they lack the "right stuff."

This book encourages and supports women in their steep climbs to develop their influence in line with their values and to realize their ambitions. I also aim to extend the influence of mentors, as they better discern what handrails and access to elevators would most benefit their junior women colleagues.

Implementing insights and expanding capacities begins with experimenting with new behaviors. Questions to stimulate reflection and action dot each chapter. I recommend starting a document

---

1. Stephen Jay Gould, *The Mismeasure of Man* (New York: W. W. Norton & Company, 1981).

or using a notebook for tracking what deserves more thought or for stream-of-consciousness writing on what's intriguing or troubling.

If, like me, befriending yourself has not come naturally, you might imagine an older, more companionable version of yourself asking the questions. Or, since hearts and minds are often in conflict, you might set up an inner conversation—between for example your risk-taker and your security-seeker—and see what emerges. Ideally a wise thinking partner is available to dialogue on questions of mutual interest.

The origin of the word *develop* is *dis-envelop*—that is, to unfold and unfurl, to open up whatever scripts are interfering with living and working out of our strengths and values. As we unfold into our unique potentials, we increasingly access the wisdom of our own inner coach and friend. This book is a full-service resource on this empowerment.

PART 1

FOCUSING INWARD

PART 1: FOCUSING INWARD

CHAPTER 1

BUILD ON YOUR STRENGTHS

Self-discovery is really hard work. Maybe that is
why so few people do it and why so few people are
really great human beings and great leaders.
—Richard Boyatzis

No one can make you feel inferior without your consent.
—Eleanor Roosevelt

▶ *Focus on strengths rather than on weaknesses.*
▶ *Since overdoing a strength turns it into a weakness, take steps to prevent this tipping point.*
▶ *Obtain constructive feedback to close gaps between your intentions and your actual impact.*

Self-discovery sounds easy. After all, what is more fascinating than oneself? Usually, however, we prefer to examine other people. And can we ever fully know ourselves? Our copious self-involvement and lingering defense structures limit a full-on intersection with reality. Our fathomless unconscious remains unconscious. And doesn't everyone have at least one behavior that they'd rather not look at too closely? A great deal of evidence has accumulated that self-deception is built into our biological and social design[2] (Chapter 5). So even at our most self-aware, we are always partly opaque to ourselves. Therefore, whatever we can do to advance a realistic assessment deserves investigation.

Discover and Build on Strengths

Our talents, a reflection of our strongest synaptic connections, reveal themselves in our yearnings (what activities we look forward to), rapid learnings (what focuses come easily), and satisfactions (what's fulfilling and fun). *Flow* is an energized focus state that happens when our whole being feels involved, and we don't want to be doing anything else, because our interests and talents are meshing perfectly with a challenging activity.[3]

Psychologist Mihaly Csikszentmihalyi, who investigated and named the psychological concept of flow state, observed that achieving flow usually depends on *years of practice* to reach high levels of competence and agility. Paying attention to what enables this energized focus guides us in creating optimal conditions and identifying activities worthy of us.

We tend to know ourselves more by our shortcomings than by our strengths—probably because we prefer to hide our limitations. So it comes as great news that we grow faster by focusing on our strengths rather than on what we dread. To be sure, an awareness of our weaknesses and vulnerabilities is also important (Chapter 2). We'll always face situations that require us to engage in mortal combat with our limitations. But as we gain the power to choose, we can move toward activities that we both enjoy and are good at rather than trying to get better at what we'll never be good

---

2. Shankar Vedantam, *Useful Delusions: The Power and Paradox of the Self-Deceiving Brain* (W. W. Norton & Company, 2021).

3. Mihaly Csikszentmihalyi, *Creativity: Flow and the Psychology of Discovery and Invention* (Harper, 2013).

at. We can form functional partnerships with those who are skilled in the areas we are not; and, if we have the resources, we can hire out what doesn't fit us. All of this greatly expands our opportunities for flow.

Questions for Reflection

▶ Which of your talents reveal themselves in your yearnings (what activities you look forward to), rapid learnings (what focuses come easily), and satisfactions (what's fulfilling and fun)?

▶ What are you learning about encouraging the flow state of your interests and talents meshing perfectly with a challenging activity?

▶ How do you interpret the observation that responsibilities attach to our strengths?

The Myers–Briggs Type Indicator (MBTI)[4] and CliftonStrengths Assessment[5] (formerly StrengthsFinder) are two helpful instruments in the continuing work of building on strengths.

Myers-Briggs Type Indicator (MBTI)

The MBTI is a tool that uses four scales to help people understand their communication and interaction preferences. The MBTI is often misapplied and poorly taught, and it's less useful to those who score toward the middle of the scales. But for most people, it creates a picture of our innate ways of perceiving the world and making decisions, and this has multiple uses, including *insights into the strengths we take for granted*. The four scales are:

---

4. My expertise with the Myers–Briggs Type Indicator derives from certification to administer this instrument, familiarity with C. G. Jung's writings on psychology on which this instrument is based, and decades of using this tool.

5. Gallup, "CliftonStrengths," https://www.gallup.com/cliftonstrengths/en/home.aspx.

1. *Introversion* (energy focused inward) or *Extraversion* (energy focused outward).
2. *Sensing* (taking in information via the senses) or *Intuition* (taking in information via the imagination).
3. *Thinking* (making decisions through analysis) or *Feeling* (making decisions with our values and heart).
4. *Judging* (plan- and structure-oriented) or *Perceiving* (flexible and seeking more information).

We all use all these functions and orientations every day, but most of us habitually lean toward one end of each scale. Those with strong preferences get really good at using them, in the same way that we get really good at using our preferred hand.

In broad terms, *Extraverts* are always ready to talk; *Introverts* bring the gift of depth. *Sensers* are good with details and reading instruments; *Intuiters* imagine alternatives. *Thinkers* offer logic; *Feelers* connect with people. *Judgers* are organized; *Perceivers* are more flexible and spontaneous.

One letter from each category produces a four-letter label, resulting in sixteen "types." These types are grouped into four temperaments: ST = rule-oriented guardians; NF = people-oriented idealists; SP = doing-oriented artisans; NT = strategy-oriented rationals.

I can be described as an ENFJ (Extraversion, Intuition, Feeling, Judging). I communicate easily and enthusiastically (Extraversion), listen with my imagination (Intuition), make heart-led (Feeling) decisions, and am always on time and well-organized (Judging). I will never enjoy discussing theory (Thinking preference) or rise above being pitiful at navigating the details of websites or at fixing anything (Sensing strengths).

A few more generalizations about the scales may be useful. Extraverts seek to express themselves, offering a vocal diagram of their inner workings. Push a button, and ten stories emerge. Even as Extraverts focus on others, they tend to promote themselves and to wish for recognition. Introverts' attention is directed toward understanding what they are perceiving. They remain on guard against others' explanations and external claims.[6] Introverts don't speak until they have something to say and find Extraverts annoying when they repeat what's already been said. Introverts learn to reserve energy for the social gatherings essential to networking and arrive with bridge-building questions (for example, "What changes in your field are you most concerned about?").

People with Judging (organized) and Perceiving (flexible) orientations toward life need each other. Js enjoy making decisions and prefer order. Many Ps find decision-making stressful and like to keep their options open, believing that critical information is around the corner. While Js seem to get more done, because Ps are more open-minded, Ps have better capacity to handle uncertainty and sense what's emerging—increasingly important skills.

The only scale showing a gender difference is Feeling, which is not surprising, given eons-old cultural expectations that women put relationships first. Women who combine Introversion and Thinking (true, for instance, of most scientists) may find that their focused expression when concentrating may be misinterpreted as anger (hence the term "resting bitch face").

As our familiarity with MBTI terminology increases, we may be able to "type" others. When we find it difficult to connect with someone, we'll likely find differences on a couple of these scales. Knowing our preferences gives us insights into how we are similar

---

6. June Singer, *Boundaries of the Soul: The Practice of Jung's Psychology* (Anchor, 1972).

to or different from others and enables versatility. We can adapt our style so that others relate to us more easily. For instance, Introverts understand me better if I allow more pauses and use fewer words than is my wont. To influence a Thinker, I reduce my natural animation and choose words like "analyze" and "strategize" over more enthusiastic verbs. Good counselors, negotiators, and mediators are skilled at this kind of mirroring, easing the way to a meeting of minds.

None of the applications discussed here pigeonhole people. On the contrary, this instrument offers a nonjudgmental language for understanding personality and communication differences.

C. G. Jung's theory of personality development (on which the MBTI is based) posits that we are designed to grow more whole as we mature. As we come to understand the limitations of our innate preferences, we reach more of our potential if we deliberately work with our non-preferences. For instance, in order to write, I must increase access to my analytic capacities and to my deepest Introverted energies. If I don't give myself relationship-free solitude, my energies will keep extraverting, and my values will pull me to attune to others. Often our favorite hobbies rejuvenatingly draw on non-preferred functions. For instance, birdwatching, gardening, and biking nail me to the here and now (Perceiving) in my senses (Sensing).

Questions for Reflection

▶ Using MBTI language, name your innate strengths. What are you using as evidence? Bounce your responses off someone who knows you really well.

▶ How might you take even better advantage of these strengths?

▶ How might it serve you to practice more with your non-preferences?

The CliftonStrengths Assessment

The CliftonStrengths Assessment (formerly StrengthsFinder) can be useful at the beginning of a career, during job transitions, and for those seeking a fresh look at their strengths. This assessment presents pairs of statements, sorts them, and reflects dominant patterns or "signature themes." For example, my five signature themes are: achiever, strategic, communication, learner, and input.

The assessment's descriptions of these categories prompt invaluable reflection on how overdoing a strength just a little bit begets a weakness. *Input* indicates that I'm good at collecting information on what interests me—that is, the infinite variety and complexity of the universe. But I tend to go overboard. Instead of doing the much harder work of analyzing and synthesizing, I keep collecting. The discipline of frequently summarizing and sorting what I'm taking in prevents my writing projects from collapsing into chaos.

Overdoing Preferences and Strengths

In part because they remain invisible to us, we are inevitably going to overdo our preferences and strengths. Those who are loyal may be exploited. The highly empathic may unconsciously absorb others' anxieties. The generous may become resentful if their gifts are not reciprocated. The self-reliant struggle with collaborations. Perfectionists hold themselves and others to impossible standards. Super-strivers over-function in the areas of their passions. Those who pride themselves on their sense of responsibility forget to ask for help. We are all *too something* for our own good.

As author and philosopher Alain de Botton notes, "Every strength of character we admire bears with it a weakness we must forgive."[7]

---

7. Alain de Botton, *The School of Life: An Emotional Education* (Penguin, 2019).

Questions for Reflection

▶ Which of your strengths do you tend to over-apply until they tip into a weakness? What conditions are at play? What disciplines or supports might help prevent a tipping?

▶ How do you interpret Alexis de Tocqueville's observation: "We succeed at enterprises that demand the positive qualities we possess, but we excel in those that can also make use of our defects"?

Obtaining Feedback

Paradoxically, self-knowledge depends on asking others for their perceptions of us. But many people do not receive the kind of feedback that boosts accurate self-confidence. Few parents are skilled at providing this to their children. I received almost none while growing up and craved affirmation, delaying my ability to affirm myself.

On the other hand, getting too much praise may delay self-efficacy, especially if it's useless ("Great job jumping into the pool ... holding the door open ... eating your pizza!"). Further, Carol Dweck's research on *fixed* mindset versus *growth* mindset demonstrates that children who are praised only for specific abilities may develop a sense of self-worth contingent upon a specific outcome and then hesitate to take on new challenges. Alternatively, children who are encouraged for their *efforts* develop an understanding of how they can grow their abilities.[8]

It's our responsibility to procure the feedback we need to close gaps between our excellent intentions and the actual impact of our words and actions. The more influence we wish to have, the more

---

8. Carol Dweck, *Mindset: The New Psychology of Success* (Ballantine Books, 2006).

necessary this is. This fact comes as bad news to almost everyone. The question, "Can I offer you some feedback?" may generate a fight-flight-freeze response in the brain. Some professionals manage to create a self-reinforcing feedback-free zone such that they never hear critiques of their behaviors, compromising the effectiveness of any team, partnership, or collaboration in which they participate. Allowing in information about how we can improve entails pushing through uncomfortable feelings of vulnerability. That's why I know feedback to be the breakfast of champions.

Questions for Reflection

▶ What was your experience with feedback growing up? More recently?

In the Workplace

Asking our buddies general questions about how we can do better won't get us what we need. Most friends and colleagues feel unqualified to help. Others, unskilled at these kinds of conversations, may unthinkingly lob a zinger that damages the relationship. Giving useful feedback in a tactful, absorbable way is a highly-evolved skill.

Soliciting feedback in a workplace that lacks a sense of collegiality and safety will yield little value. But when collegiality prevails, we can ask for specific feedback from colleagues who are qualified to rate the skills we are trying to improve.[9]

Since we all need support and affirmation as well as critiques and challenges to keep growing, we should ask about strengths

---

9. See especially: Marshall Goldsmith, *What Got You Here Won't Get You There* (Hyperion, 2007), and Douglas Stone and Sheila Heen, *Thanks for the Feedback: The Science and Art of Receiving Feedback Well* (Viking, 2014).

and about areas for improvement. For example: "What would you say I'm especially good at? Do you have observations on when I could dial these strengths up? When I need to dial them down?" Or: "I'm working at improving my communication skills. If you have thoughts on what I'm already good at, or about how I can be a better listener, will you share them?"

We can also name problems we suspect. For example, "In what ways do you see me over-functioning (for example, micromanaging) or under-functioning (for example, avoiding awkward conversations)? How is this behavior impacting our work and relationship?"

One of the most sensitive areas on which to seek feedback regards self-presentation: how our physical presence and demeanor feel to others. We might ask: "Do I have any mannerisms or vocal tics that detract from my effectiveness? Anything about my appearance or self-presentation that I might try to adjust? How do I come across on Zoom?"

We can also be alert to opportunities to get on-the-spot feedback, such as after a meeting: "Any observations on how that went? What could I have handled better?" Because initiating such conversations feels awkward, a good opener may be: "I'm aware of my own discomfort in asking these questions, but I hope you'll be as candid as possible." And then we do our best to resist even the slightest urge to correct or argue with the feedback-giver. We often learn the most from unsolicited feedback, although as the saying goes, "Criticism is hard to take, especially from a boss, friend, family member, or stranger."

Even if feedback is hard to hear and to interpret, input from any trustworthy person without a bone to pick is a gift, and we should treat it with respect. We try on difficult feedback we receive, perhaps asking a few friends for their interpretation of its validity. Sometimes we need to sit with it for a while. Sometimes the feedback just doesn't fit. After all, others are sharing their perceptions based on their values and limited experience of us. We listen for themes that are arriving from multiple sources.

In addition to feedback providing potentially invaluable guidance, seeking feedback also demonstrates a commitment to our own growth, communicates our respect of those we ask, and models courageous conversations. As we can, we would all do well to offer each other more specific encouragement.

Questions for Reflection

▶ What behaviors and skills could you use feedback on? What's a first step? What's hardest about this? What might help?

▶ Have you been avoiding giving feedback to a colleague or a direct report who might really benefit from it? If so, what's preventing you from meeting your responsibility to this person?

▶ To whom might you give some encouragement and positive feedback?

Why Women Often Underestimate Themselves

Women who give the impression of being too big for their britches face grave penalties. To avoid being accused of bragging, women tend to overcompensate in the direction of modesty, inadvertently downplaying their expertise—a kind of protective hesitation.[10] This socialized tendency means that women are less likely to get credit for their work when it counts, feeding a negative loop of underpayment, underestimation, and self-doubt. Some men express confusion as to

---

10. Linda Austin, *What's Holding You Back? Eight Critical Choices for Women's Success* (Basic Books, 2000).

why their superb women colleagues seem to lack the confidence to advocate for themselves, unaware of the risks women may take when they do so.[11]

Simultaneously, women often take their strengths for granted, as if anybody could do whatever they're good at. One idea is for departments to host occasional "shameless self-promotion" lunches to give women practice in comfortably drawing attention to their accomplishments. I've met few women who can't use help with this. I still need help sometimes.

Women exacerbate this challenge when they attribute their successes to good luck. I've frequently interrupted women who say, "I was lucky to ..." by asking why they are minimizing all the hard work, intelligence, and sacrifice that went into the result they've achieved. This kind of conditioned humility slows developing confidence and finding worthy roles.

Additionally, many women hold themselves to impossible standards, as if anything less than perfect is suboptimal. As a result of such culture-inculcated self-doubt, women seldom apply for jobs unless they meet almost all the criteria, whereas for men, meeting a bit more than half is often sufficient. Men are also more likely to walk into their annual evaluation meeting asking for support for their next promotion. Women are more likely to confess, "I may not be ready. Plus, I can't seem to get to the paperwork." Women tend to be their own worst critics, putting themselves down before anyone else can—complicit in their own silencing.

Further compounding these disadvantages, women must exercise more caution than men in requesting and interpreting feedback. A self-confident colleague might misinterpret a woman asking, "How

---

11. Janet Bickel, "How Men Can Excel as Mentors of Women," *Academic Medicine* 89 (2014):1100-1102.

do you think my talk went?" as insecurity. Worse, women tend to receive more negative feedback even when their performance is equivalent to men's, and the feedback is usually focused on impressions of appearance and personality ("unattractive," "abrasive," "bubbly"). Such demeaning comments reflect the narrower band of assertive behaviors that most men and women allow women before dismissing or condemning them (Appendix 1).

At the same time, I've found that women are more forthcoming in asking how they can do better. Unaccustomed to critical feedback, many men get defensive. Women with lots of experience in subordinate positions are accustomed to hearing about how they need to improve.

Given the difficulties women face in claiming their strengths, mentors and colleagues can do more to affirm women's ambitions and capacities for influence. A simple reminder or observation can have a lasting impact in helping someone internalize the evidence of her value and impact.

Questions for Reflection

▶ Have you known girls or women who struggle with internalizing the evidence of their strengths? How do you interpret this difficulty?
▶ Looking back, do you find evidence of underestimating yourself? In what ways might you still be underestimating yourself?

Imposter Syndrome

Nothing is more energizing than self-confidence. But self-generated messages of personal incompetence often plague highly committed professionals. Some high achievers suffer from imposter syndrome—that is, they are successful by external standards but have an illusion of personal incompetence. Despite a solid record, they worry that they have deceived others into thinking they are competent. This delusion feeds a perfectionism that masquerades as a virtue. But being driven by what people think subverts the risk-taking necessary to experimentation and growth. Plus, as author Rebecca Solnit notes, "The perfect is not only the enemy of the good; it's also the enemy of the realistic and the fun."[12]

Recovery starts by comparing the *evidence* of accomplishments to the *evidence* of incompetence and irresponsibility. When feeling overwhelmed by both our own and others' expectations, we do what we can to take ourselves off the hook a bit and accept that sometimes we will disappoint others as well as ourselves. We discover the meaning of "good enough." If debilitating self-doubts continue, a professional can support our developing accurate reference points and a goal-focus rather than a gap-focus.

For those times when my inner critic is repeating, "Another thing that's wrong with you is…," I list to myself what I'm grateful for, shifting my focus to the positive. I also keep a folder labeled "Joy" with reminders of meaningful contributions and of others' faith in me. Of course, sometimes I forget all of this. I take Chögyam Trungpa's observation to heart, though: "A great deal of chaos in the world occurs because people don't appreciate themselves. Having never developed sympathy or gentleness towards themselves, they do not experience harmony or peace, and therefore, what they project to others is also inharmonious and confused."[13] Developing sympathy and gentleness toward ourselves depends on facing our fears, the subject of the next chapter.

12. Rebecca Solnit, *The Mother of All Questions* (Haymarket Books, 2017).
13. Chögyam Trungpa, *Shambhala: The Sacred Path of the Warrior* (Shambhala, 2007).

CHAPTER 2

LEARN FROM YOUR FEARS

It's deeply poignant that we should expend so much effort
on trying to look strong ... when it's really only ever the
revelation of our somewhat embarrassing, sad, and
anxious bits that renders us endearing to others.
—Alain de Botton

The curious paradox is that when I accept myself
just as I am, then I can change.
—Carl Rogers

▶ *Gain release from your inner critic by compassionately looking
your fears right in the eye.*
▶ *Replace uncharitable self-assessments with evidence of your continuing resourcefulness and capacities for growth.*

No matter how smart we are, our fears limit our access to our
best selves. It is much easier—and human—to focus on
others' behaviors than to face the fears at the root of our lifelong
internal struggles, as the two case examples in this chapter illustrate.

Ultimately, though, avoidant behaviors create problems that can be fixed only by changing our own actions.

"I have been getting angry when anyone asks me to do something more than I'm already doing—which is a lot," Miriam told me. She was one of my coaching clients and a division chief at a busy health care institution. "Patients can be so unrealistic, and my trainees think they know more than I do. In addition, my boss, for whom I have bent over backward, keeps expecting me to see more patients. So last night when my husband asked for help with his computer, I got pissed—I want to say, not on top of everything else. No one knows all the responsibilities my work entails."

"It's no wonder you're feeling distressed," I replied. "How have you been taking care of yourself?"

"I've been noticing how righteous and indignant I feel. This gets in the way, like we talked about last time."

"Yes, righteous indignation lets off steam but interferes with our assessing individual situations. How about timing the number of minutes you allow yourself to indulge in this feeling? These kinds of emotions are an indicator of burnout, as I'm sure you know. You've been running flat out in the service of all these people for a long time. It's hard to know how to stand up for yourself sometimes, isn't it?"

"I just thought this transition into part-time as a first step to retirement would be easier," Miriam said. "I want to set up a graceful transition and to be remembered as a caring leader. If I start saying no—as I must, in order to completely retire in two years, given our heavy patient load—other people will think of me as a quitter."

"Let's generate some ways you might reframe this dilemma for yourself," I offered. "For instance, you have been solving everyone's problems for a long time. People are addicted to your reliability. How can you wean them off your dependable responsiveness?"

"You're right. When someone asks for help, I have been there to fix the problem! I've got to stop doing this all the time for my own good."

"So, what is the first step?"

"I need to send a different signal."

"What will be hardest about sending a clear signal as to your more limited availability? How will you manage to draw and then hold a new line?"

"I don't want to disappoint anybody. I have been a people-pleaser for as long as I can remember."

"Many of us share this type of response, and it can be a liability. But it's never too late to begin setting firmer boundaries. When we're clear about our own goals, we send clearer signals to others. How about trying some free-association writing to discover more about the tensions between your preferences and the pressing expectations of others? Listen for emerging themes; for instance, when you feel like a martyr and are internalizing others' disappointment. Try to be curious about, and kinder to, yourself."

Miriam was coming to see how early in life she had opted to stay small rather than to set and hold boundaries, and how she had accumulated resentments by placing her own needs last. Now she feared that even after decades of service and leadership, her contributions would remain unappreciated. She made progress putting her own goals first from here on in, communicating her priorities confidently, and getting comfortable with others' disappointment.

In this second case study, Jasmine had adopted a pleasing but inauthentic persona that she used to avoid difficult conversations. She opened our first session with:

"I contacted you because I've just accepted a big promotion at another institution that comes with a much better package than I have now. Here's the immediate problem: When I told my boss and the head of my mentoring team, I expected that they would say, 'Congrats,' or, 'Is there a change we could make that would make you want to stay?' or, 'How could we have better supported you?' Instead, they went ballistic and accused me of playing them. They said, 'We hired and trained you, and this is how you repay us?' And it's gotten worse: now they're retaliating and making it as hard as possible to make a smooth transition. I've heard lies being spread about me."

"That sounds intense. How are you interpreting all this?"

"I guess I knew that my boss and my mentor would be hurt that I am leaving, but their anger has me tied in knots."

"In what ways might you have contributed to how this is unfolding? Are you ready to look at this?"

"Mainly, I am trying to figure out how to survive this retaliation and make a smooth transition into this big new leadership role."

"I understand. At the same time, growth depends on our discerning and accepting responsibility for the role we have played in what has happened in any important relationship."

"But at this point, with my back against the wall, I can't admit any weaknesses to my boss."

"So, then just between us, when you look back, do you have any ideas on how any of this ill-will might have been prevented?"

"Well, my relationships with my boss and my mentor have always been friendly. But I never felt like I had the right to disagree to their faces. Sometimes I just let them think I agreed rather than being totally honest. I could tell they thought they were investing in me, and I let them think so. I've always deferred to authority figures, I guess—and then done my own thing—and I've accomplished so much! I've always tried hard to please others."

"How are other members of your team adapting to your news?"

"I can see now I was sending mixed messages, like, 'We're in this together, you're my team'—and now I'm saying, 'I'm ready to move on.' I've been sleepless over how hurt some of them feel. Given what's happened, I can see where I might have handled things differently. I know I need to own my part in some of this."

Gradually, Jasmine accepted responsibility for the consequences of her approach and committed to proactively facing conflicts and initiating sensitive discussions.

Self-Centered Fears

Fear inevitably arises at the interface of the known and unknown. Alain de Botton writes, "Anxiety is a reasonable and sensitive response to the genuine strangeness and riskiness of existence ... a justifiable expression of our mysterious participation in a disordered, uncertain world."[14] It feels increasingly normal to harbor multiple environmental, global, national, and local fears—in addition to what often feel like uniquely personal ones. David Foster Wallace says, "Everybody is identical in their secret unspoken belief that way deep down they are different from everyone else." Yet when it comes to our fears, as private as they feel, we can bet that we are not alone.

Self-centered fears tend to fall into two categories: fears we'll lose something we already have, and fears we'll fail to get something we feel we deserve.[15] Our fears whisper, "You deserve better" or "No one suffers as much as you do" or "You're hopeless." A trance of scarcity[16]—a false assumption that there won't be enough

---

14. de Botton, *School of Life*.

15. Paraphrased from Alcoholics Anonymous's *Twelve Steps and Twelve Traditions*, Step 7.

16. Victoria Castle, *The Trance of Scarcity: Stop Holding Your Breath and Start Living Your Life* (Sagacious Press, 2007)

of whatever we need that cripples us from acting, a kind of chronic FOMO—bolsters these judgmental voices.

Since fears usually present as enemies, our instinct is to avoid going behind the lines. But if we don't investigate what's alarming us, the fear wins. Some fears are False Evidence Appearing Real—that is, junk that our imagination has manufactured and that doesn't deserve our attention. To differentiate between fears that are benign and those that may cause us to self-sabotage, we must get to know the enemies hiding in our negative feelings. In this never pleasant work, it helps to remember that, as myth and legend speak of, treasure lies where we falter and stumble. The poet Rumi encouraged: "Don't turn away. Keep looking at the bandaged places. That's where the light enters you."

Vulnerability

Brené Brown's groundbreaking study of vulnerability has guided many of us in the courageous work of putting our fears under a microscope.[17] Brown describes vulnerability as that "unstable feeling we get when we step out of our comfort zone." We feel vulnerable when there's any possibility of failure, rejection, or threats to our feeling competent and in charge. These could come from job hunting, moving, changing disciplines, traveling, the unexpected jolts of everyday life.

We seem to be hardwired to conceal feelings of vulnerability. Humans are mammals needing years of care from birth; perhaps we never recover from the oceanic vulnerability of infanthood and the fear of being dropped.

---

17. Brené Brown, *Daring Greatly: How the Courage to Be Vulnerable Transforms the Way We Live, Love, Parent and Lead* (Gotham, 2012).

Our nervous systems do not distinguish between a threat to our ego and a physical threat. Both states release adrenaline that prepares us for action but lowers access to our executive functions (Chapter 4). In addition, the opioid level in our brain drops when we feel de-skilled (that is, stupid), putting us into a state of intrinsic narcotic withdrawal.[18] No wonder we prefer to stay in our comfort zones until there's no comfort left.

Shame

Connecting with others is how we become fully human. Shame impedes these connections by intimating that we are unworthy. Brené Brown teaches how shame derives its power from being unspeakable—feelings so painful that they must be shoved out of sight. But if we can approach our personal wall of shame and compassionately name what's there, we can begin a therapeutic relationship with what we find.

While nobody wants to be advised that they need professional assistance, many people do need help to overcome negative internally-generated messages. I certainly did.

As I began this inner work, I noticed how my "shoulds" were always wagging a big forefinger at me: "You should be better at this" or "You should be busy all the time." When I gained weight after I quit smoking, my favorite pair of jeans started making me miserable. Recognizing the insanity of giving an item of now useless clothing that much power, I cut them up. After that breakthrough, a giant red "Wrong Way" sign began guiding me when other "should"-spewing metrics would arise. It's great news that we can get better at choosing our route through our old internal maps.

---

18. Anthony L. Suchman, "Uncertainty, Competence and Opioids," *Journal of General Internal Medicine* 20 (2005): 554–555.

Questions for Reflection

▶ What internalized voices of judgment are you most aware of? What triggers them?

▶ When repetitive rumination over a mistake or disappointment takes over, what are the stories you're commonly telling yourself? What evidence can you summon that contradicts your story? Who might help you see the bigger picture?

▶ What minor embarrassments is it time to completely let go of? In what other ways might you lighten up on yourself?

Replace Uncharitable Self-Assessments

As we become familiar with our fear habits, we encounter parts of ourselves that feel inferior.[19] Although these elements are not hardwired, these voices seem to come from deep inside us, and when we're vulnerable, they push us around as if they own us. But our inferiority complexes did not originate inside of us. That children imperceptibly internalize their loudest critics feels to me like a tragically universal design flaw.

Sometimes these voices present as powerful members of an invisible committee. Psychiatrist Bessel van der Kolk recommends this analogy: Each of us is like a family in which the members have different levels of excitability, maturity, wisdom, and pain. (I would add addictive tendencies to this list.) Getting along with ourselves depends on how well we're listening to and taking care of our different family members.[20] When different parts of who we are have

---

19. Mark Epstein, *The Trauma of Everyday Life* (Penguin Books, 2014).

20. Bessel van der Kolk, *The Body Keeps the Score: Brain, Mind and Body in the Healing of Trauma* (Penguin Books, 2014).

been warring for a long time, we may need a counselor's assistance in negotiating a peace.

James Hillman, a psychoanalyst and author, notes that the care we give any humiliating part of ourselves is also the cure, and that "caring sometimes means ... the ability to carry it along."[21] Once we gain freedom from the weight of any attendant shame, we feel more companionable toward ourselves. Then our self-doubts, unsolvable tensions, unhelpful tendencies, and surprising fragilities no longer feel so burdensome.

Questions for Reflection

▶ What might an empathic friend say about how you're taking care of your inner family?

▶ What self-improvement projects deserve to be given up (at least for now)?

The Alternative of Staying Small

The natural state of mammals is to be somewhat on guard. We all develop defenses to help us survive the powerlessness of childhood. Some defenses reveal themselves in psychosomatic symptoms like a nervous stomach. Some children cope via the comfort of a blanket or thumb.

For defenses that are harder to treat or outgrow, the "loyal soldier"[22] analogy can be helpful. Our "loyal soldier" is the courageous,

---

21. James Hillman, *The Force of Character and the Lasting Life* (Ballantine Books, 2000).

22. This image derives from Japanese soldiers who needed help adjusting after their country surrendered in World War II; their communities created a ritual of publicly thanking and discharging these soldiers, assuring them that now that the war was over, they should return home as welcomed citizens. See: Bill Plotkin, *Soulcraft: Crossing into the Mysteries of Nature and Psyche* (New World Library, 2003).

stubborn part of our personality that helped us survive the vulner-abilities of childhood. For some, our loyal soldier's approach was to make us small so that we were sufficiently acceptable to authority figures. Tactics may have included self-criticism, perfectionism, placing our preferences last so as not to displease, inauthentic personas, social withdrawal to minimize hurtful contact, and repressing sensuality, emotions, and intelligence.

My thumb, literally resembling a little soldier, effectively soothed me through childhood (although I paid with lifelong dental issues and extraordinary difficulty weaning myself off cigarettes). My soldier was also all about being "good." This meant suppressing my fears and intelligence no matter how upset or bored I was.

As we recognize that our adult self possesses resources that our worried child did not, we can thank our soldier for her years of protection and then retire her. Gradually, we see that there's nothing to defend or to prove and no authority figures to obey or to please. I have found the Enneagram valuable in recognizing my predictable patterns of vulnerabilities, constrictions, and defenses. (See the end of this chapter.)

If we have grown up in a family or in a body in which we felt like we did not belong, we may require help dismantling our layers of protective shields. Originally, these defenses represented a positive effort to adapt, to seek safety. But this suit of armor becomes a disability, hampering our ability to learn and to trust ourselves and subsequently others.

We progress by experimenting with new behaviors, which usually opens us to fresh perspectives. For instance, at the end of my first year in business, I dreaded sending out invoices. I felt that some clients had not received sufficient value for their investment despite my best efforts. Out of this discomfort I hit upon the idea of accompanying invoices with a collection of thought-provoking and entertaining quotes gathered from my voracious reading. As I've continued to expand my compilation and share it more widely, my end-of-year collection has become quite popular and is widely forwarded—illustrating how a practice that originated in vulnerability may generate an unforeseeable abundance.

As we try out different responses to old triggers, our brains establish the new connections fundamental to behavior change. Anyone who has worked to quit smoking or overeating knows how much help, courage, and perseverance this takes. The obvious fact that we're responsible for our own rewiring isn't usually a sufficient motivator. Ultimately, achieving escape velocity from internally- and culturally-generated constrictions depends on our living a life that is rooted in our own values (Chapter 3).

Questions for Reflection

> ▶ If you identify with the loyal soldier analogy, what fresh light does this offer for gaining freedom from automatic defenses?
>
> ▶ What bad habits tend to interfere with changes you want to make?
>
> ▶ If you are still judging yourself for a vulnerability or weakness that you would never judge a friend for, how might you lighten up on yourself?

Lessons Learning

When I first started my business, I was so anxious that I didn't sleep well for over a year. To both calm and embolden myself, when I entered my new home office, I would imagine myself as a lion-tamer and proclaim, "Down, Simba!"[23] Or, I'd go swing in my hammock,

---

23. Tip from Annie Dillard.

the "no fear" zone I'd created where my demons couldn't follow me. And I started doing push-ups.

Out of desperation to keep from repeating humiliating mistakes, I created a "Lessons Learned" document[24] in which I articulated where I went wrong and what assumptions were leading me astray. Every time I added something, I would read what was already there until it could be safely deleted. I have since renamed this document "Lessons Learn*ing*," as some things are an ongoing work in progress. This practice also teaches me to differentiate between useless self-criticism and useful reminders; for example, that mistakes are part of the dues we pay for a full life, as Sophia Loren said.

Questions for Reflection

▶ What belongs in your "Lessons Learning" file?

▶ What are less self-critical ways of looking at what isn't staying learned?

▶ If your self-expectations (or others' expectations of you) keep rising, what would help you to right-size them?

Forging compassionate inner connections is how we become larger than our fears and able to operate from a more spacious identity.[25] As we accept how radically imperfect and unsolvable we are, we interpret our foibles with greater benevolence. A warmer gen-

---

24. Examples from my file: * Once a fee is agreed upon, write down what's been decided. Jeez! And stop negotiating against yourself! * Big blank spaces in your calendar are NOT a mark of failure. * Allow potential clients to tell you why they are calling and ask questions to learn more versus nervously guessing.

25. Pema Chödrön, *When Things Fall Apart: Heart Advice for Difficult Times* (Shambhala, 2016).

erosity toward ourselves unleashes access to our innate openness, creativity, and strengths.

In the Buddhist tradition, a warrior-sage befriends her vulnerabilities, manifests compassion for herself and others, deals head-on with suffering, and brings light into the world through courageous action. The first step is not being afraid of ourselves.

Addendum: The Enneagram

The Enneagram[26] is a theory of personality based on contemporary psychology combined with ancient wisdom shared by many spiritual traditions. This theory posits that each person has a central preoccupation created by our way of paying attention, and from this, a network of automatic preferences and tendencies follow. The Enneagram (*Ennea* is Greek for *nine*) identifies nine patterns. These predictable patterns are so intricately woven into our personalities that they feel normal no matter how constricting they are.

The Enneagram teaches that we are all an overstatement in one direction. I am a Seven (Enthusiast/Optimist).[27] The unconscious childhood message for Sevens is, "It's not okay to depend on anyone for anything." (Since my sister's birth when I was a toddler, I have lived as if this were true. I don't recall asking for anybody's help with anything but learning to tie my shoes.) Learning that the basic fear of Sevens is being trapped in pain or deprived of something essential came as a huge relief. My whole

---

26. For a more detailed summary: https://www.enneagraminstitute.com/how-the-enneagram-system-works.

27. One: Perfectionist/Reformer; Two: Giver/Helper; Three: Achiever/Performer; Four: Individualist/Connoisseur; Five: Observer/Investigator; Six: Questioner/Loyalist/Worrier; Seven: Enthusiast/Optimist; Eight: Boss/Challenger; Nine: Mediator/Peacemaker.

life up until then, I had assumed that my fears of pain and scarcity were neuroses unique to me.

To avoid pain and boredom, Sevens plan new experiences, try to make everything fun, and scan for a wider slice of the sky and for ever more possibilities (queue my theme song: "Don't Fence Me In"). Expecting to be an instant expert is also a Sevens-related feature. Since recognizing this, I put less pressure on myself to deliver a workshop on short notice or to summarize a book after one exposure to the material.

The Enneagram teaches that Sevens grow by fully attending to and savoring what is here now and being nourished by present experiences rather than focusing on what's next. The deeper I delve into this interpretation, the freer I have become of my personality's constrictions—although we never gain complete freedom from our automatic patterns.[28] Familiarity with the other eight patterns also enhances my effectiveness as a friend and a coach.

Here is my take on an extremely compressed summary of the Enneagram patterns. I add one note: Many people notice that they also share some characteristics with one of their "wings"—that is, the type on either side of theirs.[29]

One: Perfectionist/Reformer: pays most attention to rules and standards; maintains a rigid sense of responsibility; evidence of growth: leaving something that needs fixing alone with no sense of angst or restlessness.

Two: Giver/Helper: focuses singularly on what others need; generosity may backfire into resentment; evidence of growth: attending to their own needs first.

---

28. Richard Rohr, *Enneagram II: Advancing Spiritual Discernment* (Crossroad, 1995).

29. The two books most useful to me in composing this summary: Don Richard Riso and Russ Hudson, *The Wisdom of the Enneagram: The Complete Guide to Psychological and Spiritual Growth for the Nine Personality Types* (Bantam, 1999) and Roxanne Howe-Murphy, *Deep Coaching: Using the Enneagram as a Catalyst for Change* (Enneagram Press, 2006).

Three: Achiever/Performer: driven to compete in every aspect of life; evidence of growth: engaging in an experience for its own sake with no need for outcome or product.

Four: Individualist/Connoisseur: feels above normal aspects of life; longs to be appreciated for their aesthetic tastes; evidence of growth: taking specific steps toward tangible outcomes.

Five: Observer/Investigator: researches constantly and so procrastinates, especially if anything social is involved; evidence of growth: more contact with their body and other human beings; greater ease with decisions and action.

Six: Questioner/Loyalist/Worrier: looks for guarantees of security/stability; evidence of growth: following their own inner guidance and lightening up on themselves and others.

Seven: Enthusiast/Optimist: seeks ways to avoid pain and boredom; evidence of growth: being nourished by present experiences rather than focusing on what's next.

Eight: Boss/Challenger: super-sensitivity to power differences; anger is close to surface; evidence of growth: experiencing and expressing caring, vulnerable feelings.

Nine: Mediator/Peacemaker: avoids conflicts; often silent; difficulty putting feelings into words so denies or pretties up feelings; evidence of growth: engaging with rather than avoiding difficulties in relationships and in communicating.

PART 1: FOCUSING INWARD

CHAPTER 3

DEFINE SUCCESS FOR YOURSELF

No one will ever create a bolder vision of your life
than you are able to envision for yourself.
—Linda S. Austin, MD

Three things are needed for people to be happy in their
work: they must be fit for it, must not do too much of it,
and must have a sense of success in it.
—John Ruskin

▶ *Pursue subjects that fascinate you.*
▶ *Avoid the traps of seeking security, applying invalid metrics to your progress, comparing yourself to others, and fearing failure.*
▶ *Accept that dips in confidence and clarity are common, even during mid-career.*

An accurate estimation of our strengths guides us in defining success for ourselves (Chapter 1). Belief in our capacity for growth and agency is also essential. Most of us are born with a drive to realize ourselves with increasing intensity and scope. For those raised to put others' needs before their own, however, setting and staying connected to self-generated goals may seem less important and come less naturally. Until only a few decades ago, women were discouraged "for their own good" from formulating any notion of success for themselves beyond caring for their families. Although women now have comparatively more freedom to pursue individual goals, societal expectations and relational responsibilities add layers of struggle that few men experience in developing self-efficacy and agency (Appendix 1).

A Moving Target

What success means to us often morphs as we gain in experience. I've known several faculty members who strove for decades toward the award of tenure only to discover that they had banked their ladder against the wrong tree, as the rewards in no way compensated them for all their sacrifices. This disconnect brings to mind a cartoon in which one knight says to another: "Wait, the Holy Grail is just a cup? We've been traveling all this time to locate a cup?"

We see a wide range of orientations to success. At first, success may mean being able to find a job and pay the bills and interest on student debt. For some, the question of success doesn't pop into terrifying relevance until they're anticipating their first big college reunion. Some hard-core strivers never stop chasing the brass ring of an authority figure's view of success. Self-directed entrepreneurs, motivated by the ability to work on their own terms, are oriented toward what success in their industry looks like. Artists often face extra challenges in identifying relevant reference points for success and how they will fund it.[30]

---

30. William Deresiewicz, *The Death of the Artist: How Creators Are Struggling to Survive in the Age of Billionaires and Big Tech* (Henry Holt and Co., 2020).

Finding where our talents meet the world's needs in a way that also puts bread and protein on the table begins with *pursuing subjects that we find exciting*, and then searching for ways to gain ever more experience with these areas. As Abraham Lincoln advised: "Whatever you do, be good at it."

However, regardless of how competent we become, cycles of steep climbs, signless crossroads, and feeling stuck or lost are natural. Dips in confidence and clarity are common. If we can accept that self-doubt accompanies new ventures and difficult tasks, we're less likely to expect a particular trajectory or to imagine that there is one "right" way.

Questions for Reflection

▶ What has life been teaching you lately about success?

▶ How might your expectations of a career "path" be unrealistic?

For Young Professionals

In career development presentations to young professionals, I often introduce this topic by asking them to close their eyes and consider, "What images arise when I ask: What does success mean to you?"

Your personal and professional hopes probably intertwine and include widely varying emphases: as much autonomy as possible along with satisfying and non-codependent relationships; a sense of competence in, and pleasure from, daily activities; opportunities to keep building skills; living somewhere you enjoy, and likely a host of others. These hopes are likely accompanied by anxiety about how you'll be able to accomplish your preferred combination.

Whatever your take on success, you are the CEO of your career. Accepting responsibility for being the creative force in your life means living on your own terms versus living a life defined by others. If you looked at your career as a business with a mission and a budget, you would access the best guidance you could find and strategize based on your assessment of emerging opportunities and constraints. You would try to approach this often uncomfortable process with the same curiosity you bring to whatever most interests you in life.

Ikigai is a Japanese concept that embodies the idea of happiness as the sum of small joys in everyday life and the ability to look forward to the future even if you're miserable right now. In the West, this concept has come to be associated with a Venn diagram composed of four overlapping qualities—what you love, what you're good at, what you can be paid for, and what the world needs—with ikigai representing the intersection of these four circles. Both iterations of ikigai can serve as excellent guides to prospering.

Success Traps

Continuing to grow in the direction of your strengths and values gets easier as you gain familiarity with your vulnerabilities and counterproductive tendencies, and as your expertise and network of colleagues grow. While there's no formula for locating ikigai, an awareness of common success traps can prevent you from getting stuck. Here are some of the most common traps:

Seeking security:

Helen Keller said that security is mostly a superstition. Any sense of security you cobble together is a function of your skills and solid relationships. These keep expanding only if you are taking wise risks in the directions you want to be going. Psychologist Abraham Maslow observed: "You will either step forward into growth, or back into safety."[31]

Some who manage an early big success assume they've got it made until something interrupts their assumed trajectory. Naturally, we occasionally long for a secure niche, especially with regard to finances, but locating one that keeps bringing in money has been shown to be mainly a matter of privilege and lucky timing.

It's also helpful to remember that insecurity is not the opposite of security. When we take risks on behalf of big goals, intervals of insecurity naturally arise; as we work through them, they come as less of a surprise and are less troubling.

Overdependence on goals and plans:

Ideally, your goals pull you forward and function as guides to prioritizing—so long as you don't pointlessly beat yourself up if you don't meet them. Not everyone needs goals to stay motivated. If they constrict your ability to notice emerging opportunities and constraints, plans and goals you fall in love with can restrain rather than advance your growth.

Other people's definitions of success:

From childhood on, we are likely to receive often contradictory messages about success, beginning with our family- and cultural-specific versions of "success." Common messages are: "failure is not an option"; "get a 'proper' job," "family first," and so on. To sort through these messages on the way to becoming the CEO of their own life and career, many need to leave home.

---

31. Abraham Maslow, *A Theory of Human Motivation* (Martino Fine Books, 2013).

Other people's metrics also arrive in the form of standardized tests and performance evaluations. These may provide useful affirmation and information but are based on databases and values that may not fit you. If these measures feel invalid or unfair, take a close look at the gaps between what's expected and what you're capable of. Ditto if you feel constant pressure to prove your worthiness. If you're not meeting your own or anybody else's expectations, wise friends or counselors can help you interpret the gaps and find useful indications of progress.

Social media also present dangers. Many young people are curating a persona, favoring the unreal over what is real about their bodies and minds, without paying attention to the steep prices that inauthenticity exacts down the line. As Anne Morrow Lindbergh said: "The most exhausting thing in life is being insincere."

Unrealistic metrics:

High grades in school lead some to assume that they'll continue to ace all subsequent endeavors no matter how severe the competition or how high the bar. Another deceptive aspect of high grades is that they don't necessarily indicate that actual learning has occurred.

An overfocus on money is also common. Decades of studies of college students reveal increasingly unrealistic expectations regarding what they can earn, how they should look, and what they should own. It is to be hoped that those focused on materialistic values before long come to see that relationships hold life's greatest blessings.

Comparing yourself to others:

As children, when comparing ourselves to friends and frenemies, we always seem to come up short. To compare is usually to despair, and this tendency can be hard to unlearn. A key insight for me arrived in a crowded lounge as I nervously awaited the arrival of a potential client. Everyone else looked so much happier and more self-assured than I was feeling. By comparing my contorted insides with others' put-together outsides, I'd cornered myself into an acute angle of misery. Over time, as I noticed how such comparisons undermined my self-confidence, I got better at hopping off any train of association that subtracted from the validity of my own reality and from the evidence of my own expertise.

On the other hand, when others inspire you, remember that you wouldn't even notice that admirable trait unless you already possessed some of it. Dzigar Kongtrul writes: "When we appreciate others' significant qualities, it is as if we have lassoed these with our recognition and pulled them closer to enrich ourselves."[32] As you seek out the company of and develop relationships with admirable people, you become richer and richer. I have also learned the hard way not to put anyone on a pedestal. Not only is this always a recipe for disappointment, but the statue also blocks my view of where I need to go.

Fear of failure:

Failure and success are not opposites. Innovative people experience more failures because they pursue more ideas and opportunities. Any success is the result of dozens of usually hidden false starts and dead ends, especially in science. Renowned physicist Niels Bohr claimed, "An expert is a person who has made all the mistakes that can be made in a very narrow field." Science writer Stuart Firestein finds that: "Failure is the default. Success requires an unusual conflu-

---

32. Dzigar Kongtrul, *Light Comes Through: Buddhist Teachings on Awakening to Our Natural Intelligence* (Shambhala, 2009).

ence of events in which entropy is temporarily reversed. In science you not only have to have the stomach for failure, you actually have to enjoy the taste of it."

Some days it may seem that there are tons more ways to fail than to succeed. What is important is that you get to decide for yourself the meaning of the event and where it fits into your emerging journey. When you don't get the break or the job you were longing for, mine it for clues: Is this evidence that the role was not a good fit? That your model of the world is in error? That you need a different approach altogether?

We all need help from time to time to keep a healthy perspective. One idea is for department heads to host an occasional "failure party" to which people bring examples of their rejected projects, grants or papers and state what they've learned. As Confucius said: "If you make a mistake and do not correct it, that is called a mistake." Seek out those who have also gotten their ass kicked and who have carried on. Failures, especially when they occur in pursuit of your goals, can teach you exactly what you most need to learn.

Because failures tear at our hearts as well as our egos, a whole raft of negative feelings may arise. We learn what we can and then we move on, accepting that disappointments cluster near the heart of human experience and that the consensus of leaders and philosophers across time and cultures is that our failures are often our most reliable teachers. These life lessons smart, but I haven't found any other way to get smarter.

Questions for Reflection

▶ Which of these success traps have been, or are, most difficult for you to avoid? What are you learning?

▶ What plans and goals might it serve you to hold more lightly?

▶ What is life teaching you about failure?

▶ How do you interpret writer Kathryn Schulz's proposition: "We are wrong about what it means to be wrong.... Mistakes enable not only our biological evolution but our social, emotional, and intellectual evolution as well"?[33]

Generate Your Own Definition of Success

As we come to terms with the world's metrics for success and get clearer about our own strengths and priorities, we come closer to our own definition of success. There will certainly be intervals where we're just trying to survive. Yet by learning from and addressing the obstacles we encounter, if we're fortunate, we can gradually combine what's satisfying in the short term with what benefits us in the long term as well.

The following decision criteria assist careful assessment of opportunities as they arise:

▶ How does this opportunity align with my strengths? Immediate goals? Long-term goals?

▶ Is this essential to my success right now in this role? (If your answer doesn't align with your boss's answer, how might you find a middle ground?)

▶ Will this put gas in my tank or deplete my energy?

▶ Is this a one-time-only opportunity, or will I likely be asked again? (In other words, will this ball bounce back to me at some point, or will it self-destruct if I don't catch it?)

▶ Where will the time required for this activity come from? What trade-offs will this necessitate?

---

33. Kathryn Schulz, *Being Wrong: Adventures in the Margin of Error* (HarperCollins, 2010).

- ▶ What impact am I likely to have? Is it worth the effort?
- ▶ What time frame does the commitment require?
- ▶ If resources, credit, or visibility is important, do I need to negotiate anything up front?
- ▶ Would taking this on mean compromising something I've already promised?
- ▶ Who is asking? How important is this relationship? If I say no, would that jeopardize our relationship? Or would the bigger risk be to say yes and then not meet the commitment?

As demands on us increase in line with our skills, we tend to expect more of ourselves. But if we're constantly disappointing ourselves, we're unable to maintain the positive self-image on which our energy depends.

It is necessary to our sanity to accept that life, especially now with so many sources of distress and uncertainty, will continue to present challenges to our sense of mastery. When we find ourselves in despair over all we cannot influence, we're listening to the wrong voices.

Mid-Career

Dante famously began his epic: "Midway along the journey of life, I woke to find myself in a dark wood where the true way was wholly lost." However common the experience of losing one's way has been throughout history, it's still a shock when it suddenly happens to us. We tend to expect that our chosen path will go as far as we wish. We forget that all animals must fight for their optimal habitat.[34]

---

34 . Catherine Raven, *Fox and I: An Uncommon Friendship* (Spiegel and Grau, 2021).

Mid-career professionals must reckon with many forces that influence whether they can continue to develop their talents in line with their values. This turbulence and ambivalence, often stimulated by a desire for more autonomy, are normal and not an indication of a personal deficit.

A common dilemma is whether to step out of a role that has taken years of hard work to acquire but is no longer a good fit. Acknowledging, rather than denying, our ambivalence helps us identify and evaluate options. We see with greater clarity what values we're negotiating between. We poke at our past and current images of success and see what emerges about our motives and sacrifices.

In evaluating options, helpful questions include:

▶ Have my ideals, or the intensity of my beliefs or devotion to my ideals, changed over time (or since I started this career path/job)? If so, how?

▶ What misalignments have developed between my priorities and my responsibilities? What misalignments can I live with, and which require action?

▶ How do I decrease involvement in activities that are not a good fit? What commitments can I renegotiate?

▶ How can I reserve more energy for the people I care about and for personal health and rejuvenation practices? What are the likely trade-offs?

▶ How can I regain a sense of momentum and generate fresh ideas?

▶ Do I need to relocate, seek more training, or shift emphases? Who might help me with these reassessments?

Questions for Reflection

▶ What is the boldest vision of your life that you can envision for yourself? Ideally, how would you apportion your time?

- ▶ How important is autonomy to you, and what are you willing to sacrifice to have more?
- ▶ How do you define riches?
- ▶ What redistribution of energy deserves consideration? What can you put less of yourself into?

As we mature, we see how good decisions are the result of experiences we've learned from, and how these experiences are usually the result of bad decisions. This being so, who is to say which were truly bad and which good? Life keeps teaching us what we most need to learn. Our whys keep us wise. The closer we can stay to *why* we're doing what we're doing, the more educated our choices and trade-offs will be.

Author and leader David Whyte teaches that if we stay open to the transforming possibilities of our relationships and our work, our ambitions and our failures metamorphose into a generosity and compassion for ourselves and for others. These actionable feelings of generosity and compassion have come to underlie my definition of success, as has his conclusion: "The greatest legacy we can leave is to pass on a sense of the sheer privilege of having found a road, a way to follow, and then having been allowed to walk it."[35]

Questions for Reflection

- ▶ How do you interpret/apply these observations?
  - ▷ "If you want a quality, act as if you already have it."—William James
  - ▷ "Success is to be measured not by the position that one has reached in life as by the obstacles which have been overcome."—Booker T. Washington

---

35. David Whyte, *Crossing the Unknown Sea: Work as a Pilgrimage of Identity* (Riverhead Books, 2001).

CHAPTER 4

INCREASE YOUR EMOTIONAL INTELLIGENCE

The more clearly you understand yourself and your
emotions, the more you become a lover of what is.
—Spinoza

▶ *Have your feelings instead of your feelings having you.*

▶ *When you feel devalued or challenged, pause, exhale slowly, and
ask: "What hooked me?"*

▶ *Positive emotions widen receptiveness to the unexpected.*

Healthy relationships depend on understanding our own and
others' emotions.[36] The most useful way I've found to define high
emotional intelligence (EI) is: The ability to identify our feelings as they
arise, to connect our personal experiences with those of others, and to
remain open and centered even when we feel devalued and challenged.
The more complex the work, the more dependent on others we are to
get something done, the higher the degree of stress, the more EI matters.

---

36. Definitions of emotions and their intelligent use abound, beginning with Daniel
Goleman, *Emotional Intelligence: Why It Can Matter More Than IQ* (Bantam,
2005) and, most recently, Brené Brown, *Atlas of the Heart: Mapping Meaningful
Connection and the Language of Human Experience* (Random House, 2021).

Unlike IQ, we *can* improve our EI—a lot. No matter where on the scale we begin, we can get better at "having our feelings" instead of our feelings "having us."

When it comes to emotional maturity, children whose parents were sensitive to their signals and who mirrored them get a big head start, especially when parent and child also give each other considerable freedom to interrupt and modify interactions without losing touch with one another, and when the child learns effective means of self-soothing.[37]

It wasn't until I was almost sixty that I finally got to witness high EI in action. I was co-leading a challenging leadership retreat with a colleague who engaged the tense group with just the right mix of humor and humility, who showed confidence in the group's ability to meet its goals, and who skillfully approached all differences and conflicts as natural opportunities for learning.[38] I almost wept—both with joy for the gift of this inspiring colleague and with sadness that I'd lived so long without access to such a good example of high EI.

Background on Emotions

Human emotions are ancient, laid down far earlier than language, and sculpted by the realities of survival. Our affective content, most of which remains unprocessed within us, is largely housed in the limbic system. This collection of structures assigns feelings to the information streaming in through our senses, decides how much value to give this information, and determines what we remember.

---

37. Daniel J. Siegel, *The Developing Mind: How Relationships and the Brain Interact to Shape Who We Are* (Guildford, 1999).

38. Anthony L. Suchman, MD, Principal, Relationship Centered Health Care (see also *Thanks*).

Hence, contrary to Dr. Spock, our emotions are the foundation of reason—not the opposite of it.

Most complex tasks have both emotional and cognitive components, and usually these parts of the psyche collaborate. But when our survival is at stake, the limbic system is all about self-preservation. At the first hint of threat, adrenaline increases blood flow to muscles to prepare for fight or flight. Under these conditions, the reason-oriented rider only marginally controls the strong horse of the emotions. An equally valid analogy is that affect is in the driver's seat, and rationality is a passenger offering lucid suggestions for slowing down and rethinking the route.

These days threats to our egos exponentially outnumber threats to our physical safety. But until the rider/driver gets emotionally smarter, a small pump of envy or anger may still prime our horse to charge. Even a tiny release of blood pressure–elevating adrenaline constricts blood flow to the cerebral cortex, reducing access to logic, and it stays active in the body for hours. Fortunately, unless accompanied by adrenaline, the half-life of our quicksilver emotions is so brief that if we don't feed them, they reliably fade.

Emotions, with all their unpredictable fluctuations, are as contagious as viruses. Our exquisite nervous systems are designed to communicate with those of other mammals. The upsides of our permeability are evident when we are in harmony. Has someone's smile ever improved your day? When we smile, not only does our body relax and release endorphins, but others may also "catch" our good mood. When we observe an act of kindness, we're more likely to act kindly. And the kinder a person is, the more kindness she tends to find in other people.

A darker consequence is that when we suppress anger, not only does our own blood pressure increase but so does the blood pressure of those observing us. And as we know, repeatedly suppressing anger ensures that it will burst forth at the worst time. Anger, anxiety, angst, and angina all come from the same root, meaning *to constrict*. Another downside of suppressing emotions is that this effort pulls us out of the present where our attention needs to be and impairs our memory of events.

Strong emotions contain a lot of information. Positive ones like joy feel like the whole point of life. Uncomfortable emotions alert us to difficulties that deserve our attention. Anguish that has remained buried for a long time, maybe over generations, requires the help of a professional to unpack.

Working with formless and chaotic emotions often begins with finding words for them. It is tragic that so many men are socialized to keep their emotions at bay such that they remain unable to identify and effectively communicate their feelings. Without language for their feelings of sadness or anxiety, many men default to expressions of anger or impatience—obscuring the originating problem and often creating new problems for the people around them.

Overcoming cultural and familial conditioning takes support and exposure to skilled examples of communicating difficult feelings. It benefits us all to patiently help each other along here (Chapter 6).

Questions for Reflection

▶ If you grew up with emotionally mature and empathic parents and teachers, how would you describe their strengths and what you learned from them?

▶ What is your experience with suppressing your own anger?

▶ What is your experience with helping those accustomed to keeping their emotions at bay to begin to constructively express them?

My Learning Process

I've found no better way to illustrate EI concepts and possibilities than through my own learning experience. My early life didn't provide practice with working through difficult emotions. A frown was likely to be met with, "What if your face froze like that?" and tears with, "I'll give you something to cry about."

Fast-forward a couple of decades: Ten years into marriage, my husband and I needed help working through some emotional issues. We were fortunate to find an excellent marriage counselor who, by the way, espoused that marriage is a miracle. The truth of Alain de Botton's observation that, "Before you are married, you can live under the illusion that you are easy to live with," became clear to me for the first time. She helped me begin to see how everything that irritates me about others can teach me something I need to understand about myself.

In order to take accurate responsibility for problems I have with people (no matter how hard they are to get along with!), I began examining exchanges that irritated or disturbed me: Is this part of a pattern? What story am I telling myself about it? Do I feel like a victim, martyr, or hero, or all three? If it seems advisable to revisit an unfortunate exchange with someone, I also ask myself: What are my motives, and what are the possible risks of raising this issue?

Assessment Instrument

Soon after starting my coaching business, I became certified in a reliable EI assessment instrument, now called the WE-Q Profile.[39]

---

39. You can learn more about this instrument here: https://learning-in-action. teachable.com/p/eqprofile-experience. This instrument assessment includes videotaped scenarios depicting tense boss/employee conflicts followed by questions eliciting responses to the scenarios.

I needed more help than self-debriefings could provide, and I was also intent on offering another service to my clients. In this section, I describe my scores on the instrument scales in some detail to encourage readers to reflect on these scales themselves.

I showed a high level of fitness on *accurate empathy* and *compassionate empathy*. Empathy is how we bend our time to walk in step with others. Accurate empathy is the ability to tune in to others and guess what they are experiencing. Those who grow up with an unpredictable parent often develop this capacity. Compassionate empathy is the further ability to meet people where they are and to walk in another's shoes, experiencing their reality without needing to change them—a capacity key to coaching, mentoring, parenting. Arrogance, fear and fatigue interfere with compassionate empathy.

I also scored high on *balanced reliance on thoughts, feelings, and wants*. Life keeps helping me further develop this balance. For instance, I once invited my husband to join me hiking in an area that I'd previously enjoyed in solitude. When his impatience with parking began to infect me, I checked in with my thoughts ("He's making a big deal out of nothing"), my feelings ("I'm regretting inviting him"), and my wants ("I want to have a good time together"). Since this last component was the most desirable, I chose to switch gears in this direction.

I scored low on *access to a full range of feelings*. I showed much higher access to fear and anxiety than to positive emotions. Since I feel happy most of the time, these results confused me until I remembered that *the purpose of this instrument is to illuminate what happens in difficult work and personal situations*. Since emotions drive most of our actions and decisions, access to the whole human range of them heightens our understanding of others, especially when the going gets tough.

Positive–negative orientation (that is, optimism combined with realistic assessment of events) was another low-scoring area for me. When I feel devalued, I am much more likely to arrive at a negative than a positive interpretation of a situation, as might be predicted by the sin-oriented Lutheran–Missouri Synod tradition of my upbringing.

My low score on the scale of *self–other balance* (easily accessing our own needs and experience while also focusing on another person without losing touch with ourselves) helped me understand how, early on in my coaching, I would insecurely lean in so hard to what my clients were saying that I lost touch with my own expertise.

The *self-regulation* component of the instrument identifies four relationship strategies: high trust in self and in others (excellent EI); high trust in self and low trust in others ("my way or the highway"); low trust in self and high trust in others (easily giving others authority); and low trust in self and in others. Ideally, during stressful interactions, we maintain high trust both in ourselves and in others. I showed a tendency to lose trust in both.

At first, because they didn't fit my own self-assessments and the test's scenarios didn't fit my experience, I rejected all my low scores. But shortly after obtaining this profile, I went to a doctor's appointment, only to find that I was not on their schedule. Noticing my heart pounding, I took a deep breath. I recognized how automatically I lost trust both in myself ("Is it my fault?") *and* in the busy radiology office ("How could they do this to me?"). As I analyzed my reaction, I reminded myself that I had insufficient evidence for a wholesale loss of trust in myself or in this office and that appointment mix-ups happen to almost everyone. Not being stuck in the center of my own universe, I could learn a different way to respond. As I have worked with these insights, and with my clients on their results, I've come to appreciate the value of these EI constructs.

My subsequent participation in two relationship-oriented fellowships[40] has also boosted my capacities to go toward rather than shy away from relational tensions and to hold them lightly, to notice how the way we show up influences others, and to develop courageous presence.[41] The best professional development programs now offer some assistance along these lines.

Questions for Reflection

- ▶ Think about how you respond under trying conditions and rate your fitness on:
  - ▷ Accurate empathy.
  - ▷ Compassionate empathy.
  - ▷ Balanced reliance on your thoughts, feelings, and wants.
  - ▷ Maintaining a balance between yourself and the other person.
  - ▷ Trusting in yourself and the other person.
- ▶ Relive a scene in which your response to a challenge dismayed you. Which of these EI scales are helpful to understanding your response?
- ▶ If you're low on Empathy in troubling situations, start with trying to be *curious* about what another is feeling, and try that feeling on.
- ▶ Think of a time when you lost trust in yourself. What were the circumstances? What are you learning about bolstering your self-trust? When should you question whether your judgment is trustworthy?

---

40. *The Courage to Lead* program created by Penny Williamson, ScD (an internationally recognized facilitator, organizational consultant, educator, and coach), based on the revolutionary work of educator Parker J. Palmer (at the Center for Courage and Renewal); and *Leading Organizations to Health*, led by Anthony L. Suchman, MD and Diane Rawlins, Relationship Centered Health Care Principals (See *Thanks*).

41. Nicole A. Steckler, Diane Rawlins, Penelope Williamson, and Anthony L. Suchman, "Preparing to Lead Change: An Innovative Curriculum Integrating Theory, Group Skills and Authentic Presence," *Healthcare* 4 (2016): 247–251.

Applications

Increasing the intelligent use of our emotions serves us in every avenue of life. Here are what I've found to be the most useful applications of the above constructs:

The instant we detect any intimate signal from our body (for example, speeding heart rate, rising heat, shoulders tensed up to our earrings), we are receiving a one-time-only invitation to examine what has triggered that reaction. Pause, take a deep breath, exhale slowly, and, with compassionate curiosity, ask yourself: "What hooked me?" "Why am I reacting so strongly?" "What has gotten me anxious or upset right now?"

This pause for reflection gives us a chance to catch up with ourselves, to refresh and reframe, and to learn from our discomfort rather than to automatically dismiss it. Slowing down to breathe mindfully also makes physiological coherence possible, therapeutically connecting mind and body. For instance, I notice when I'm feeling contracted and can shift into a more expansive mode. As Lily Tomlin quipped: "For fast-acting relief, try slowing down."

Often emotions first register as vague sensations or tensions that may be worthwhile to investigate. For instance, if I feel excitement or dread, I ask myself what I need to be cautious about. Exploring a restlessness, a mood, or an imbalance in eccentric detail may yield a bit of therapeutic light or even a poem.

Ideally, we move among our thoughts, wants, and feelings with something approaching a balance. Some patterns are predictable. Those who rely heavily on *wants* tend to be action-oriented, but in their drive, they often disregard their impact on others. People who tend toward *thoughts* may miss emotional clues, and those strong on *feelings* may be hijacked by their emotions.

Sometimes an even keel will be beyond us, especially at home. At work we're performing a role, and our social selves set boundaries. Dust-ups are more common when we're freer with our vocabulary; inaccurate accusations slip out ("you never/always"). If we can learn to pause, we see what's triggering our automatic defenses; gradually we become less reactive, remaining centered in situations that used to end in yelling.

Finally, context and time of day can make a big difference. Beloved meditation teacher Thich Nhat Hanh noted: "It's funny how much our surroundings influence our emotions. Our joys and sorrows, likes and dislikes are colored by our environment so much that often we just let our surroundings dictate our course."

Questions for Reflection

▶ If there is a challenging situation on your horizon, what emotions are likely to arise? What are your goals for handling this situation?

▶ What's hardest for you about pausing to reflect when you feel challenged?

We aim for equipoise—that is, the ability to serenely monitor the movements of the mind and correct for biases as they arise—even though we know we will often fall short. We know we are making progress when we can prevent the birds flying over our head (which we can't change) from building nests in our hair.

Emotions respond much like muscles: the ones most frequently stimulated become strongest. Positive emotions open the mind—we see and recall more, and our maps of the world grow richer. Pessimism shrinks our focus. Positivity widens our attention and our receptiveness to the unexpected.

It's great news that as we move into our sixties, the areas of the brain that produce and regulate emotional response grow calmer.[42] As the mind quiets and our fears lessen, we attend better to our own intuition. Our humility and humor more readily win out over selfishness and touchiness. We pay more attention to positive experiences. As our ability to integrate cognitive and emotional intelligence expands, we better tolerate ambiguities and tensions, easing the work of seeing through the assumptions that cloud our perceptions of ourselves and of the world (Chapter 5).

---

42. Wray Herbert, *On Second Thought: Outsmarting Your Mind's Hardwired Habits* (Crown, 2011).

PART 1: FOCUSING INWARD

CHAPTER 5

IMPROVE YOUR OBJECTIVITY

People with clear minds are like magnets.
—Wilma Mankiller

If others examine themselves attentively, as I do, they would
find themselves, as I do, full of inanity and nonsense ....
Those who are aware of it are a little better off.
—Montaigne

▶ *Recognize how our brains oversimplify everything.*
▶ *Slow down to examine assumptions.*
▶ *Notice false dichotomies such as masculine/feminine, white/
non-white, etc.*
▶ *Highlight opportunities to expand the pie.*

The better we understand how our brains function, the more
deliberately we can work toward accuracy and objectivity. Smart
decision-making depends on our ability to question our assumptions
and beliefs. Flooded as we are now with information as well as
disinformation, this work of discernment is becoming harder and
ever more important. It's not only science-deniers and generators

of "alternative facts" who add to our difficulties here. High levels of expertise and narcissism also affix myopia-inducing lenses. Personal wealth evidently generates cultural amnesia and many self-justifying delusions.[43] Plus, interacting with an electronic device creates a world in our own image: "I see. I find what I know. I enjoy this recognition of myself."[44]

Become Aware of Cognitive Shortcuts

The mind creates the universe in which it lives. To make sense of our world, humans simplify the complex information streaming in from our senses. So "what is unsought will go undetected," as Sophocles noted twenty-five hundred years ago.

Just as we hear and see within a narrow and survival-enhancing range, so do we think. Nobel Prize–winning psychologist Daniel Kahneman explains that we function via cognitive shortcuts and perceptual filters.[45] The brain, attempting to predict what's going to happen next, builds an oversimplified model of the world. We're hardwired with a strong inclination toward "excessive coherence" and a primal aversion to confusion. That is, we tend to suppress evidence about what we can't make sense of and to embrace information that supports what we've already concluded. Our preferences and aversions narrow our perceptions.

Our normal state is to have intuitive feelings and opinions about almost everything; these become beliefs. We ignore indications of our own cognitive dissonance. We want to be secure yet free, intimate yet

43. Matthew Stewart, *The 9.9 Percent: The New Aristocracy That Is Entrenching Inequality and Warping Our Culture* (Simon and Schuster, 2021).

44. Ayad Akhtar, "The singularity is here," *The Atlantic* (December 2021): 17-24.

45. Daniel Kahneman, *Thinking, Fast and Slow* (Farrar, Straus, and Giroux, 2013).

independent, successful yet rested, right but open-minded. We also unconsciously assume that we have no blind spots and that our view of reality is more accurate than other people's. Under threat, we're even more likely to fall into self-justification and me/them thinking: "I understand the situation; those who disagree with me don't."

Then there's our innate negativity bias, believed to have developed as a survival mechanism to help us pay attention to potential danger. We're at least three times more likely to notice and recall something negative than something positive—it's the difference between Velcro and Teflon.[46] Evidently, a single unpleasant remark makes a deeper impression than about five compliments combined (in marriage the ratio is even worse).[47] So, even if there are twice as many positives as negatives in our world, because of how we perceive and remember things, it may still feel like life sucks.

Moreover, as complexities increase, we save mental energy by automating whatever we can. For example, we're all recipients of thousands of culture-generated neurological downloads that enmesh people in certain roles based on appearance and historically-assigned roles. Evidently, a millisecond's worth of exposure to someone of a different race, gender, or social status activates the brain's processor of emotion. By age three, children already perceive faces of other races as being angrier than those of their own race.[48]

Decades of studies demonstrate how cognitive shortcuts under-value women. In particular, women are less likely to be presumed credible or competent. Women must demonstrate their competence again and again to be seen as equally skilled. The same behaviors for which a man is evaluated as "confident, analytic, good at details,

---

46. Jonah Lehrer, *How We Decide* (Houghton Mifflin, 2009).
47. Chade-Meng Tan, *Search Inside Yourself* (HarperOne, 2014).
48. Isabel Wilkerson, *Caste: The Origins of Our Discontents* (Random House, 2020).

open, and passionate" tend to earn a woman the labels "conceited, cold, picky, unsure, and controlling" (Appendix 1). These kinds of perceptual biases are most likely to occur when we are rushed and when we lack specific decision-making criteria—and these are the conditions under which most decisions are made.

Since we don't notice our assumptions, we seldom question them. We often don't even know in what direction our assumptions are going to be wrong, looking right when the information we need is there waiting for us on the left.

Knowing when and how to investigate our assumptions and conclusions requires a deliberate kind of processing. To accurately evaluate situations and people, we must slow down and reflect: *How* do I know what I think I know? How do I know if X is true? Otherwise, no matter how fair and rational we assume we are, our shortcuts, like invisible blinders, narrow our vision.

Questions for Reflection

- ▶ What cognitive shortcuts and perceptual erasers tend to interfere with your evaluation of situations and people?
- ▶ What gender-, skin color–, religion-, or privilege-related filters are you aware of in yourself? What's helping you notice them? How are you working free of them?

The Binary Barrier

Another innate human tendency is to notice and learn through categories, contrasts, and comparisons: self/other, left/right, awake/asleep, cold/hot, light/dark, etc. But some of our deeply ingrained either/or contrasts blind us to manifold subtleties. Reducing the world to a series of dualities—Republican/Democrat, innocence/guilt, logic/emotion—obscures a vast middle ground. As Gloria Steinem observed: "Many questions have seven or a dozen sides. Sometimes I think the only real division into two is between people who divide everything into two and those who don't."

Therefore, key to increasing the accuracy of our appraisals is detecting when our binary labels are reducing what we notice. We now see how artificial many socially constructed binaries are: masculine/feminine, homo/hetero, white/non-white. Such wildly arbitrary and migrating dichotomies interfere with understanding and respecting differences. Sexism, racism, and prejudice of all kinds are rooted in such dualisms and extend cultural power differences that limit what's possible for humankind.

An *either this or that* approach often hamstrings us. A tendency to label people as either trustworthy or not, likeable or unlikeable, etc., blinds us to how *both/and* logic is more accurate. That is, someone can be both trustworthy *and* untrustworthy, depending on the context. Like the double bind of a Chinese finger trap, we gain release by moving the fingers closer.

Polarities

Some false dichotomies are better worked with as polarities.[49] For instance, rather than thinking of individual versus community, we see that these values are interdependent in that neither stands alone. Considering them as interdependent rather than opposites puts them in dialogue, which helps us see how to maximize the upsides of what's good both for an individual and for the community.

---

49. Barry Johnson, *Polarity Management: Identifying and Managing Unsolvable Problems* (Amherst, MA: HRD Press, 1992).

Take centralization versus decentralization: The downside of centralization is excessive control; the downside of decentralization is lack of coordination. The upsides of both in balance are empowered individuals and coordinated services. Considering these interdependent qualities as polarities rather than as opposites reveals how to maximize upsides and minimize trade-offs.

Yin and yang provide another example of moving beyond binary logic to accommodate complex realities. Depicted as nestled light and dark halves of a circle, each containing a dot of the other, yin and yang demonstrate the simultaneously contrary and complementary nature of many phenomena. We have faith and doubt; we are passive and active. Similarly, the theater symbol of comedic and tragic masks expresses both delight and sorrow, bliss and suffering. Observing how seemingly opposing elements may complement and inform each other enriches our worldview.

Questions for Reflection

▶ Which of your automatic binaries may be preventing you from seeing a middle ground?

▶ Which of your traditional either/ors deserve reconsideration as polarities; that is, as interdependent variables?

Move from Fixed to Expanded Pie

"Fixed pie" or "zero-sum" logic also interferes with finding common ground. This orientation assumes that everyone is competing for a fixed number of slices such that our fortunes are inversely related: The more you get, the less is available for me—which then becomes you versus me, us versus them, with me or against me, eat or be eaten.[50] Zero-sum thinking does apply in competitions for a fixed quantity (for example, gold medals). But in most important arenas, this orientation operates with stone-age logic, such as, "All the members of my tribe have more value than any member of yours."

We can see how the fixed-pie orientation pits groups against each other. Author Heather McGhee argues that zero-sum thinking has always benefited the few at the expense of the whole. Moreover, zero-sum relies on *aversion*, eroding the very conditions under which evidence and collaboration can do their work.[51]

The first ingredient for expanding the pie is believing that we actually can—if we build the skills. Part 2 of this book covers the abilities needed to work together, including listening to each other, bridging differences, constructively handling conflict and compromises, and negotiating. As we build these skills, we will be amazed at the creativity and ability of individuals and groups to solve problems and to handle whatever emerges.

Questions for Reflection

▶ What zero-sum logic is preventing you (or a group in which you participate) from expanding a pie? What skills need to be improved?

Testing Ourselves

Familiarity with our own distortive tendencies increases our willingness to question our premises and to hold more than one inter-

---

50. Robert Wright, *Non-Zero: The Logic of Human Destiny* (Vintage, 2000).

51. Heather McGhee, *The Sum of Us All: What Racism Costs Everyone and How We Can Prosper Together* (One World, 2021).

pretation of events. Author Julia Galef recommends conducting thought experiments. For instance: If I am judging this person or group by a different standard than I would apply to another, what are my reasons? How is the context for what I'm noticing affecting my judgment? If it were someone else instead of me in this situation or difficulty, would I evaluate it differently? What would it take for me to change my view? Who might sway me?[52]

As we accept the necessity of testing ourselves on how we know what we know, we pay attention to the red flags of our doubts and surprises. To learn what we most need to from our experiences—our most valuable data source—we must probe our mistakes and uncomfortable surprises for information.

Finally, to evaluate a project accurately, it's good to decide beforehand what counts as evidence of success or failure, since unconscious self-deception is probable. Later decisions to move our goalposts are then less likely to be self-sabotaging.

Humility is likewise required. I raise my hand at Jack Kornfield's comment that "If someone whispered to us our own thoughts, we would conclude they were crazy." I appreciate Zen Buddhism's reminder of the value of beginner's mind and how leaps forward in consciousness are often preceded by surrendering the illusion that "I know."

---

52. Julia Galef, *The Scout Mindset: Why Some People See Things Clearly and Others Don't* (Piatkus, 2021).

PART 2

FOCUSING TOGETHER

PART 2: FOCUSING TOGETHER

CHAPTER 6

COMMUNICATE TO BRIDGE DIFFERENCES

Beauty is visible in moments when human beings reach
across the mystery of each other.
—Krista Tippett

The definition of warmth is how easily you convey you have
something in common with another person.
—Jessica F. Kane

▶ *Learn the basics of self-monitoring, creating an invitational presence, asking open questions, deep listening, and presenting perspectives with adequate background.*
▶ *Meet people where they are and stay open without wishing others were easier to communicate with.*
▶ *If the going gets tough, focus on identifying common ground.*

Throughout most of human evolution, we were more likely to survive if we stayed within, and shared the views of, our tribe. Now, our much more crowded and diversely-peopled world asks us to stretch ourselves in ways that seldom come naturally. Most of us find that it's easier to think alone than together. For instance, largely beneath my awareness, an elaborate narrative may be assembling in which I am the heroic protagonist. This perfect portrayal of reality does not, however, survive the first conversation at breakfast. And again, because it's so much easier, we prefer the company of those with whom we share many values. When we also have similar temperaments (Chapter 1), conversations are easy. The skills I discuss in this second part of the book are necessary only in all the other situations that a full life presents.

Because communicating across multiple differences takes multiple skills, staying in touch with why it's worth the extra work helps. *Valuing differences makes a difference by expanding what we see and can begin to understand.*[53] Philosopher and author Adam Kahane powerfully reminds us: "People who understand the concerns of others and mix those concerns with their own agenda have access to a power source denied to those who only push their own interests—to be influenced as well as to influence. Relational power is infinite and unifying."[54]

Insights into our own vulnerabilities, strengths, emotions, and assumptions (Part 1) are fundamental to getting somewhere new within any group and partnership. The bridging skills covered here are self-monitoring, creating an invitational presence, engaging in inquiry, listening, and presenting perspectives with adequate background.

---

53. Margaret Wheatley, *Who Do We Choose to Be? Facing Reality, Claiming Leadership, Restoring Sanity* (Berrett-Koehler Publishers, 2017).

54. Adam Kahane, *Power and Love: A Theory and Practice of Social Change* (Berrett-Koehler Publishers, 2010).

Self-Monitor and Create an Invitational Presence

It is humbling to note how many of the glitches we experience in relationships reflect our personal defenses, blind spots, and judgments. We applaud ourselves for our good motives and intentions while assuming those of others are not so good.

So, the most important conversations are *those we have with ourselves first.* When preparing to step into the unknown of another person when something important is at stake, we ask ourselves: What are my goals? What do I want for the relationship? What about empathy? Am I stuck in either/or thinking? Is this likely to trigger an emotional reaction? How can I prevent her from becoming defensive? We take responsibility for our feelings—for instance, "I'm feeling tense," rather than, "You're making me crazy."[55]

Another salutary practice is creating an invitational presence. Communication doesn't happen unless the other person feels invited into the conversation. Sometimes it's advisable to ask permission, as in, "Is it okay if we discuss this now?" If there's a power gap, the senior person needs to help the other feel safe. Also, those who are physically large or otherwise intimidating need to take extra steps to create the safety of a warm presence.

Questions for Reflection

▶ Can you think of a time when you launched into a sensitive subject that backfired? What "inner conversation" would have better prepared you?

---

55. Marshall Rosenberg, *Nonviolent Communication: A Language of Life* (Puddle Dancer Press, 2015).

▶ For an upcoming difficult conversation, how will you to create an invitational presence? If it's necessary to communicate virtually, how will you adapt to the lack of physical proximity?

Ask Open Questions

The essence of all coaching and mentoring is discerning what questions might help others to tap into their own wisdom and to solve their own problems. Similarly, within less formal partnerships and groups, the skilled use of inquiry is the way we open windows into one another and encourage dialogue.

Questions come in many flavors:

1. Closed (elicit yes or no answers).
2. Requesting more ("please describe," "explain").
3. Clarifying ("if I understand you correctly...").
4. Redirecting ("what does everyone else think?").
5. Open-ended (see text box).[56]

All but closed questions facilitate getting somewhere new together. Good questions both stimulate reflection and convey an intent. Philosopher Simone Weil would compassionately open with, "What are you going through?" As a way of inviting another in, we might preface our query with an affirmation: "Since you contribute so much of value to our group, to ensure that our work together continues, I need to ask a somewhat awkward question ...."

---

56. The best resource I've found on this subject is: Edgar Schein, *Humble Inquiry: The Gentle Art of Asking Instead of Telling* (Berrett-Koehler Publishers, 2013).

Examples of open questions:

- ▶ How are you feeling about ...?
- ▶ What do you understand your role in this situation to be? My role?
- ▶ What is your interpretation of ...? What are you concluding at this point?
- ▶ What do you see that I don't?
- ▶ What would represent a solution that works for you?
- ▶ May I walk you through how I came to my understanding; then you can tell me more about yours?

In conversation, "why" questions tend to be interpreted as a challenge, as in: "Why on earth do you think that?" An alternative, for example, is: "Please help me understand how you arrived at that conclusion."

Even between good friends, some conversations can be difficult to initiate. If a question implicates, even tangentially, any aspect of someone's identity (for instance, their integrity, judgment, competence), care is required to avoid provoking a defensive response. Here's a useful opening: "For the sake of our relationship, which is important to me, I need to raise a sensitive issue. ... I hope you feel comfortable sharing how you're feeling about what I've just tried to say."

When someone's actions are confusing, we might approach her via questions about gaps we have observed between behaviors and espoused values. For example, "On the one hand, you do X; yet you say that Y. Can you help me understand how these connect?"

Alain de Botton suggests these methods for taking someone back to her last reasonable idea: "You were saying a minute ago that ..."; "I was fascinated when you said ..."; "Why does that particularly bother you?"[57] You may need to offer a little encouragement, perhaps an affirming nod or expression.

Body language broadcasts a lot of information, most of which we miss on virtual communications. Now that we must rely more on pixels and eyebrows, the quality of our questions is more important than ever. So is knowing when to put a smile and invitation into our voice and demeanor.

Questions for Reflection

▶ If asking open questions doesn't come naturally to you, why do you think this is? How can you gain practice with this key skill? From whom might you learn?

Listen with a Desire to Learn

Listening attentively for any length of time is an advanced communication skill, although most of us assume we're good at it. The Chinese character for listening includes not only the ears but also eyes and an open heart and open mind. What a demand—and opportunity!

At the root of not listening is assuming we already know. We tend to listen automatically, sorting quickly into categories—right/wrong, agree/disagree. Many professionals train to home in on a diagnosis or conclusion as soon as possible, and much of the time this sorting is effective. But it is critical that we sense when to slow down and ask, "What do they see that I don't?" and when to invite the other to say more. Everyone has a partial truth, and we must lean in to learn it.

---

57. de Botton, *School of Life*.

In tense situations, we can visualize a "listening field" surrounding our body—a space where words land in our presence while we consider their intent.[58] At any point, we can hit pause and request a brief time-out—just as in sports. Heifetz and Linsky recommend that, when things heat up, we "get off the dance floor and go to the balcony"—that is, we rise above the immediate action.[59] A little elevation generates new interpretations. We might ask ourselves: "What does her attitude indicate about our ability to come to an agreement right now? What am I learning about her understanding of her role and of my role? Am I too frustrated to continue right now?"

Reflective listening saves time and increases our chances of hearing what people are *not* saying. The more accurately we attune to others, the better we sense their values and uncertainties, which speeds our finding common ground.

Barriers to reflective listening are legion: multitasking, hunger, feeling rushed, habitually drawing attention to oneself, prematurely suggesting solutions, and fatigue.[60] True listening depends on alertness and an inner stability; therefore, we will often not be good at it. But we aim to slow down into this mode when it serves a goal or a relationship.

Giving someone our full attention—one of the greatest gifts we can offer another—increases trust and, usually, the value of what's shared. The other person is more likely to be more open to our views if they have felt understood and respected.

---

58. I acquired this insight from a workshop with Wendy Palmer, the founder of Leadership Embodiment and author of *The Practice of Freedom: Aikido Practices as a Spiritual Guide* and *The Intuitive Body: Discovering the Wisdom of Conscious Embodiment and Aikido.*

59. Ronald Heifetz and Marty Linsky, *Leadership on the Line: Staying Alive through the Dangers of Leading* (Harvard Business School Press, 2002).

60. It was Nietzsche who said: "When we are tired, we are attacked by ideas we conquered long ago."

Questions for Reflection

▶ What evidence do you have about when you're not good at listening?

▶ Even when you know it's important to give someone your full attention, what's generally hardest for you about this?

Present Perspectives with Adequate Background

Since others' intentions are often difficult to fathom, why do we proceed as if our own reasoning is self-evident? Often, all we are doing is expressing well-worn beliefs and opinions, and when frustrated (or socially drinking), we repeat our views more emphatically.

The key skill here is to communicate our reasoning as simply as we can. We open with our intent, "My goal in raising this is…," and if necessary follow with a bit of background, "…and here's how I arrived at this conclusion." *The more we say, the less people remember.* We carefully select details to include based on our listeners' needs (which we discover through inquiry) and our own goals.

It took me a painfully long time to realize that I am least effective when I'm trying to prove something. Speaking with too much conviction can suck the air out of the room. Most people like to arrive at their own conclusions anyway. Paradoxically, I find that it's only when I have nothing to prove that I have something to contribute. In fact, open expressions of uncertainty can be remarkably disarming, especially compared to one-upmanship: "I might be going out on a limb here, but …," or, "I could be wrong, but what do you think about …?"

Facilitate Dialogue

As we gain skills in reflective listening and inclusive communication practices, we get better at initiating important conversations, facilitating discussions of all kinds, and helping groups to get somewhere new together. Many resources are available along these lines[61]— including newly creative approaches utilizing the power of games.[62] An improv course helped me. In long-form improv ensembles, participants take whatever has been offered and build on it with, "Yes, and ...." Because they bring the action to a halt, *but* and *no* have no place in the exercise.

Here are additional suggestions that facilitate dialogue:

- ▶ Use and ask for examples. ("Tell me about a time when that happened.")
- ▶ Test assumptions and inferences. ("Perhaps we're starting from different assumptions about the goal. Here are mine. How do you see this?")
- ▶ Agree on what important terms mean. ("What is the problem we're trying to solve? To me, success would look like XYZ.")
- ▶ Know when to name a feeling. ("As I prepare to bring this up, I sense how uncomfortable I am.")

---

61.   Recommended resources: Roger M. Schwarz, Anne Davidson, Peg Carlson, et al., *The Skilled Facilitator Fieldbook: Tips, Tools and Tested Methods for Consultants, Facilitators, Managers, Trainers, and Coaches* (Jossey-Bass, 2005); William Isaacs, *Dialogue and the Art of Thinking Together* (Random House, 1999); Mary Gentile, *Giving Voice to Values: How to Speak Your Mind When You Know What's Right* (Yale U Press, 2012); Annette Simmons, *A Safe Place for Dangerous Truths: Using Dialogue to Overcome Fear and Distrust at Work* (HarperCollins, 2016).

62.   For example, an innovative approach developed by Alexandra Suchman (CEO, BarometerXP) uses games to develop facilitation and team skills, https://www.barometerxp.com/.

- Practice perspective-taking; after the other has explained something of importance, summarize their frame of reference and conclusions. ("As I understand it, you believe X. Is that correct?")

- Listen for ways to validate and then to reframe, retaining what's essential and eliminating what's unproductive. ("I understand that her action upset you. Now let's focus on next steps." "I notice you keep interrupting. I'm willing to listen but expect to be heard as well.")

- Request a do-over. ("Yesterday you shared something difficult, and I wish I had shown up in a kinder way. I'd like to try again if that's okay?")[63]

- Use add-ons. The conjunction *but* invites others to defend their previous statement. *At the same time* is more accurate. "I hear what you're saying. At the same time, I ...." You are building on, rather than short-circuiting, another person's truth.

- Sometimes what's needed is a well-oiled reverse gear. ("I was wrong.")

- Know when not to respond, especially to ridiculous or provocative statements and when you're unclear about how to proceed. ("I'm not sure why I'm having such a negative response to what you're saying. I need some time to process this before we continue. Thanks for your patience.")

- At the conclusion of an important discussion, circling back pays big dividends. ("Please let me hear how you're interpreting what we agreed on.") As George Bernard Shaw warned, "The single greatest problem in communication is the illusion that it has taken place."

---

63. This approach is also useful in job interviews: "I've thought of something else I'd like to add to my reply on that earlier question. Would it be okay if I return to that?"

Questions for Reflection

- ▶ What is your experience with trying to prove something to anyone?
- ▶ What's hardest for you about dialogue? Where will you start in gaining more practice? Who can provide a good model of these skills?

When Dialogue Doesn't Seem Achievable

Reasoning is notoriously unconvincing to those who don't agree with our values or conclusions. This is especially true when the conclusions come from those who seem better off than we are. People privileged with education and a good income tend to overlook how these advantages appear to those without them.

These days it's not unusual to find ourselves in a state of mutual incomprehension. How do we connect with those who reject credible information or who refuse to look at uncomfortable aspects of our history? It's much easier to "stay in our lane" than to attempt to open a door.

Yet, if an opportunity arises, we want to be prepared to attempt a bridge. If backgrounds differ greatly, we take it slowly. We try to identify a common interest or safe subject (such as music, pets, or hometown) and build from there—all the while presuming as little as possible.

American suffragists of the early twentieth century provide a good example. During the seven-decade battle for women's right to vote (which served as a model for subsequent cultural change movements), suffragists created cookbooks as a way to start conversations with the millions of women opposed to suffrage.[64] Engaging around

---

64. Laura Kumin, *All Stirred Up: Suffrage Cookbooks, Food and the Battle for Women's Right to Vote* (Pegasus, 2020).

any shared need—meal preparation in the case of women's suffrage—can lay the groundwork for broaching a controversial issue.

"It's a mistake to imagine that other people are not living as deeply as you," wrote author Patricia Lockwood. Similarly it's wrong to assume that others prefer small talk to dialogue that might unearth a commonality. Meaningful conversations make people happier than an exchange of banalities. So we do well to keep safe conversation starters handy, for example: Do you like animals? What kind of music or movies do you like? What makes you sad? What's your favorite time of year? What are you feeling grateful about today? We try to open a door.

We can't solve problems we don't at least try to talk about. Recently, I listened to a friend expound on a hot-button subject on which I have a radically different take. I noticed my heart starting to race. I felt de-skilled as to how to respond—until I returned to the bigger picture of the value of staying in relationship. I recognized that the ability to even have such a conversation, however one-sided it may feel, is an accomplishment; over time, our relationship has deepened.

When we find ourselves asking, "Why bother?" one answer suggested by social activist and author Meg Wheatley is: "Because it is our turn to serve the world in these particular ways, and it's not a big deal that it's so hard."[65] There may be no one more credible on this subject than leader and infectious disease expert, Dr. Anthony Fauci. In trying to understand science-deniers, he is reported as saying: "I'm always looking for the good in people, that kernel of something that's positive." He asks himself what has been "smoldering in their lives ... that needs healing." Rather than focusing on the aberrancy of their actions, he recommends "appreciating that they're suffering ... rebelling against a failing of society."[66]

---

65. Margaret Wheatley, *Perseverance: A Discipline* (Berrett-Koehler Publishers, 2010).
66. Dan Zak and Roxanne Roberts, "Anthony Fauci is up against more than a virus," *The Washington Post*, January 27, 2022, p. C3.

Questions for Reflection

- ▶ When data and reason aren't serving, what else have you tried, and what did you learn?
- ▶ Are any privileges that you enjoy because of your education and stable life that interfere with your ability to empathize with those less privileged?

Closer to Home

Interdependence depends on meeting people where they are—that is, staying open without wishing others were more like us and therefore easier to communicate with. A range of sensitive topics arises in any enduring relationship. Parents and mentors must discern on any given day what combination of support and/or challenge a young person needs. At some point, most of us want to help a friend or family member change a behavior, such as destructive gossiping or alcohol abuse. A common mistake is to reach a boiling point and then "honestly confront" someone. Preparation is necessary to laying out why we are raising an issue and specifying how someone's behavior is affecting the relationship.[67]

Another kind of emotional conversation arises from the need to gently end a relationship. All relationships morph, and there are as many reasons for growing apart as there are people. However, when mutuality has been presumed, it is deeply wounding to just be dropped. When a friend suddenly shuts us out, the resulting pain and confusion can last for years. Passively allowing someone to assume a nonexistent closeness (as people-pleasers and manipulators do) may have as cruel an impact as actively lying.

---

67. Rosenberg, *Nonviolent Communication*.

Here's one approach to signaling a shift: "This is really uncomfortable to say, but I feel like we don't have much in common anymore," or, "I'm finding less overlap in our values and interests than I used to. How do you see this? … I won't be back in touch for a while. I hope you understand that I'm not blaming you for anything."

Questions for Reflection

▶ What awkward conversation have you avoided that you are preparing to attempt? What feelings are arising?

Step up to the Plate

Life will continue to throw us into all manner of delicate situations. The path of least resistance is usually to fit in with the prevailing mood, to play it safe. Discerning whether, when, why, and how to raise a sensitive matter takes practice. Taking on these challenges, we build healthy relationships and exert a positive influence within groups and communities.

The following case study is an example of a mid-career professional stepping up to the plate:

"I'm so glad you've stayed in touch since we stopped our regular sessions," I greeted Jean. "When we spoke a year ago, you were applying the criteria I'd suggested to decide what institutional requests to say no to."

"Yes!" Jean replied. "I stopped accepting everything extra I was being asked to do. It hasn't been easy. There have been some veiled threats and attempts to blame me for things going downhill. But now I say yes only if the work or opportunity is also helping me to grow in line with my goals, especially my long overdue promotion. So I've had more time for my roles as vice-chair for research in my department and vice-chair for a major council in my society. Even though the party line is diversity and inclusion, both my institution and this professional society are still largely old white boys' clubs. I'm the first woman of color to serve in either capacity. There's no emphasis whatsoever on changing the culture. I'm struggling to figure how to raise issues of equity and process. I've seen very few good models of how to do this."

She continued: "The head of this research council is a nice guy, but he's awkward around me and is always interrupting me. I don't think he's ever partnered with a woman of color. Plus, I bring a lot more content expertise to this project than he does. Anyway, he went behind my back and inappropriately asked my friend, who'd volunteered her expertise, for more of her data, and now she's understandably backed off."

"How did you handle it?"

"I told him that approaching my colleague in this way was inappropriate and that he shouldn't contact her without getting clarity from me first. His reply was snarky, 'So you're going to let me know who I'm allowed to contact?'"

"He's probably reacting to your use of the term 'inappropriate,' which can come across as judgmental. What if you'd said something to the effect of, 'Perhaps I wasn't 100% clear about the boundaries that my colleague who's volunteering her expertise has placed around her role. What was your understanding of this? And at this point, how might you make this right?'"

"That makes sense. I'm also the only woman of color on the selection committee for this major research award. The favorite candidate was this guy who's, of course, grant-funded out the wazoo but also under criminal investigation. I finally said, 'I'm sorry, but this award is named for a woman who was a world-class leader and mentor with sterling professional ethics. Can't we award it to someone—ideally a woman—we're sure isn't going to jail?' No one picked up on my statement. The next day, I signaled I was stepping down from this committee. Evidently, this got the attention of the higher-ups. I was asked to remain and to take charge of an area that's even better aligned with my goals—we're working out the details. I do want to learn how to raise sensitive issues more effectively and to build follow-up actions into every discussion instead of everything always being left hanging."

"I'm so glad to hear all of this. First off, give yourself time to come up with a strong opening. 'I'm sorry' comes across as apologetic. How about: 'I need to raise a topic that some may find unwelcome'? And try to close with a question; for example; 'How does anybody else view this observation?' Seek role models outside your department of those skilled at raising sensitive topics and ask them how they got so good at this. And as you continue to practice these skills and build your influence, look for opportunities to get feedback on how you're coming across."

Questions for Reflection

▶ There are so few forums for practicing the bridging of sensitive differences, but we can work to ready ourselves and to create opportunities. Try initiating a dialogue with a friend using these reflective questions:

▷ How has your gender influenced your professional development? How has your skin color influenced your development?

▷ Think of a situation that revealed a gender- or race-related assumption that was in error. What did you learn?

▷ How do you interpret the phrase "white male privilege"?

▷ Cultures facilitate the participation of some subgroups more than others in self-perpetuating ways. What have you noticed about this phenomenon?

> ▷ Have you ever witnessed a misuse of power or a time when a process was derailed by prejudice? As a bystander, how might you have spoken up on behalf of the underdog?

It takes optimistic courage to build bridges as we are also walking on them.[68] The distances that separate us can feel monumental—ideological, socio-economic, ethnic, generational, geographic, faith-based. So it's therapeutic to laugh with Montaigne's observation: "It is unfortunate that wisdom forbids you to be satisfied with yourself and trust yourself, and always sends you away discontented and diffident, whereas opinionativeness and heedlessness fill their hosts with rejoicing and assurance."

However, we all share a craving to be appreciated. People generally forget what we say but not how we make them feel. Respect is like oxygen: if there isn't enough of it, that's all we can think about. Sometimes focusing on demonstrating respect is what makes the most sense.

How we show up in meetings and conversations makes all the difference in our impact on others. A courageous presence is an ethical force. When even one person in a conversation or a meeting conveys generosity or optimism, this authentic warmth may spark positive emotions in others, enhancing possibilities for working together. Since virtual communication methods limit interpersonal clues, we stay alert to when we need to apply more warmth or enthusiasm. A smile, a word of thanks, or a compliment may leave a lasting buzz. As predicted by chaos theory, small actions enable shifts that enlarge possibilities for relationship. Our words may create worlds.

---

68. Robert Quinn, *Building the Bridge as You Walk on It: A Guide to Leading Change* (Jossey-Bass, 2004).

PART 2: FOCUSING TOGETHER

CHAPTER 7

HANDLE CONFLICT AND COMPETITION WITH GREATER EASE

Conflict stirs us to observation and instigates invention
.... It is a sine qua non of reflection and ingenuity.
—John Dewey

Power is the ability to act in common.
—Hannah Arendt

▶ *Approach conflict as useful to uncovering which assumptions are shared and which are not.*
▶ *Gain practice with the conflict management style that comes least naturally to you.*
▶ *Depersonalize competitions by framing them as games where the other players are after the ball, not you.*

The skills of staying calm when challenged, examining our assumptions, and initiating dialogue reinforce each other in the handling of conflict and competition. Our temperament and upbringing also make a difference in how we approach conflict and competition.

Some of us grew up associating these facts of life with aggression and humiliation. Conflict has a bad reputation, Nobel prize winning author Toni Morrison wrote, "because we have been taught to associate it with winning and losing, with the desperate need to be right, to be alpha .... [But] conflict is a condition of intellectual life .... Firing up the mind to engage itself is precisely what the mind is for.... When it is not busy trying to know, it is in disrepair."[69]

Any two human beings will disagree on many points. But only when there is insufficient trust or respect do we label our differences a "conflict." Unfortunately, few people arrive in the workplace practiced at constructively getting differences out in the open.

Questions for Reflection

► How would you describe your experience with conflict? If discomfort predominates, what do you identify as its sources? What interpersonal differences have you unnecessarily labeled as conflicts?

Become More Versatile

Conflict management style instruments have helped many to become more flexible in addressing conflicts. One of the most well-known of these instruments is the Thomas-Kilmann Conflict Mode Instrument (TKI).

Each of us has a default mode acquired early in life. Since each conflict we face is to some extent unique, our default mode will be effective only a fraction of the time. Understanding the pros and cons

---

69. Toni Morrison, *The Source of Self-Regard: Selected Essays, Speeches, and Meditations* (Vintage International, 2020).

of each style expands our flexibility. Gaining practice with the style that comes least naturally to us helps us to become more versatile.

The five conflict management styles of the TKI are:

1. Avoiding (useful when it's not your conflict or when time will solve it, but otherwise counterproductive).
2. Directing/Competing/Asserting (goal-oriented).
3. Harmonizing/Accommodating (relationship-oriented).
4. Compromising (some of each).
5. Collaborating/Cooperating (relationship-*and*goal-oriented).

Collaborating is the only style that solves complex problems. But because collaboration takes more time and effort, is culture-dependent, and requires the most skill and humility, we underuse it. As we overcome our constricting fixed pie/zero-sum approaches and win/lose dichotomies, we see more ways to cooperate (Chapter 5).

Of these five approaches, *avoiding conflict produces the worst outcomes*. Working through difficulties together is how we come to know and trust each other. Conflict-avoiders tend to assume that harsh confrontation is their only option, which always backfires, because defenses go up. Helping relationships cannot reach their potential if one party backs away from dealing with the differences that naturally arise. This avoidance is one of many reasons why women professionals remain under-mentored (Appendix 1).

Other rampant problems caused by avoidance originate in managers' enabling poor performers by not facing up to evidence of irreconcilable gaps between employees' expected and observed behaviors. Experienced managers heed early warning signs. Combining a directive and a relational approach, they outline to the employee the evidence of the performance gap and then ask, "How do you see the situation?" If the person accepts responsibility for closing the gap, the manager and employee seek agreement on what will count as evidence of improvement and when the next review will occur. Effective delegating depends on these kinds of dialogues. Those whose default style is directive and who actually enjoy mixing things up often need to learn when to put relationships first and how to use agreement and avoidance to de-escalate disagreements.

As we lose the tendency to personalize or dread conflict, we get more comfortable with many kinds of situations. Ana had been practicing a more direct style in order to bring to her boss's attention a systems problem affecting her division's productivity. Her boss responded with, "Just calm down!" Ana is prepared to respond, "That feels dismissive. I take our team's productivity seriously. Perhaps I wasn't clear about my goal in raising this. Would you like more background?"

Questions for Reflection

▶ What is your default mode when a conflict arises? When has this approach not worked to your advantage?

▶ To become more versatile, how might you practice with the style that comes least naturally?

▶ How well did you handle the last nastygram or put-down that came your way?

Get Comfortable with Competition

Some fields and organizations feature never-ending competition for every variety of resource: salary, status, titles, space, growth opportunities, tech access, support—and even for the time and attention of bosses, colleagues, and direct reports. In many, often subtle, ways, women tend to be disadvantaged in these competitions. For instance, women are less likely than men to get credit for their contributions. A new study suggests that women scientists are less likely to be named as authors, in part because, when a project is going somewhere, the jockeying for authorship becomes so intense that only the most competitive win out.[70]

When idealists and team players find themselves in environments featuring leadership vacuums and favoring pit bulls and manipulators—a common occurrence in science and academics—many struggle to adapt to all the politically motivated games and competition. The young son of one of my colleagues gave his mom red boxing gloves for Christmas after overhearing her talking about her work.

Abraham Lincoln said, "Nearly all men can stand adversity, but if you want to test a man's character, give him power." Bullying is unfortunately common when power imbalances are acute and when management tolerates it. Methods of controlling the conversation include invalidation (for instance, labeling people, "you're unqualified," etc.) and cutting people off with sneaky attacks, such as, "I don't want to upset you but...." Successful bullies and manipulators are practiced at maintaining power over the susceptible and may even get a kick out of keeping others off balance. As our skills build, we choose whether and how to stand up for ourselves, perhaps recruiting the aid of an ally.

While power games may feel personal, they're usually just business as usual. When we personalize conflict, we're assuming that others know and care about us.[71] A more accurate framing is to

70. Matthew B. Ross, Britta M. Glennon, Raviv Murciano-Goroff, and Enrico G. Berkes, "Women Are Credited Less in Science than Are Men," *Nature* (2022), https://doi.org/10.1038/s41586-022-04966-w.

71. Don Miguel Ruiz, *The Four Agreements: A Practical Guide to Personal Freedom* (Amber-Allen Publications, 1997).

understand competitions as games in which players are chasing one another down a field. As we observe that the other players are chasing the ball, not us, we can keep our focus where it belongs: on what's happening on the field and on other players' interpretations of the "goal" and the "rules."

Staying focused on *why* we're competing enables us to shake off petty aspects of the politics and to keep our eyes on the bigger picture. When we feel constrained by events, we can make use of whatever autonomy we do have and gain pointers from those who are comfortable with competing.

If an environment feels intolerably toxic, the alternatives are to accustom ourselves to a lack of influence or to seek a more amenable culture. Skilled professionals always have options. If a move is necessary, the trade-offs are usually worth the stress of the transition because these kinds of challenges are excellent teachers.

Questions for Reflection

▶ With regard to competition, how would you characterize your field and workplace?

▶ Recall a time when you caved to a bully: What would have helped you to respond more powerfully? Project an encounter with someone you find manipulative or untrustworthy. Practice calmly responding to an insult, standing your ground, and returning to your goals for the meeting.

Gender-Linked Disadvantages

While many girls may ace academic competitions, they often lack the kind of early engagement with competition that builds confidence transferable to the work world. Nobody wins at dolls. Most boys get practice with roughing each other up and with the kind of winnable competitions they'll face in organizations. Boys are also advantaged by more freedom to express anger and frustration. Those less practiced at winning and losing tend to buckle under pressure and to back out of the kind of jockeying for recognition that typifies organizational politics (Chapter 9).

Questions for Reflection

▶ What gender-related differences in handling conflicts and competition are you aware of?

▶ As more school-age girls engage in competitive sports and other activities, do you observe this translating into skills that transfer into the workplace?

PART 2: FOCUSING TOGETHER

CHAPTER 8

NEGOTIATE FOR RESOURCES

The biggest human temptation is to settle for too little.
—Thomas Merton

Hope is not a strategy.
—George Sullivan

▶ *Generate a What's In It For Them (WIIFT). What does the other party stand to gain by negotiating with you?*
▶ *Consider the major differences in the ways you view the issues.*
▶ *Practice with a devil's advocate before tough negotiations.*

P rofessionals face both convergent and divergent needs. Negotiation is a problem-solving dialogue around these interests and needs. We seek to simultaneously meet our goals and to build a relationship whenever possible.

As the saying goes, we get what we negotiate, not what we deserve. Effective negotiating depends on relational communication skills (Chapter 6), comfort with conflict and competition (Chapter 7), and organizational savvy (Chapter 9). Adapting to new information as it emerges is also essential.

When there are many divergent interests and a lot of competition for resources, we never know what's going to turn into a negotiation. Health care professionals are continuously responding to and initiating conversations in the service of both their own needs and the often conflicting priorities of a shifting array of bosses, patients, trainees, team members, and administrators.

Formal negotiations include three phases: (1) preparation, (2) information exchange and bargaining, and (3) commitment/ implementation. This brief overview focuses on the first two stages in many types of hiring- and salary-related negotiations.[72]

Preparation

If you were socialized to not draw attention to yourself and not to talk about money, you'll need more help preparing to negotiate. Even if these difficulties don't apply to you, a good place to begin is articulating to yourself your strengths, priorities, and goals. How will you communicate these? Then sketch a Plan A (an ideal arrangement) and a couple of Plan Bs (acceptable compromises).

Next, focus on negotiating in the other party's world. This takes research and using your contacts to piece together the best picture you can. What are they looking for in an agreement? What are their priorities? Worries? What are their personal values? Management consultant and author Marshall Goldsmith notes:

---

72. Recommended resources: G. Richard Shell and Mario Moussa, *The Art of Woo: Using Persuasion to Sell Your Ideas* (Viking, 2007); G. Richard Shell, *Bargaining for Advantage: Negotiation Strategies for Reasonable* People (Viking, 1999); Kathleen Reardon, *The Skilled Negotiator: Mastering the Language of Engagement* (Doubleday, 2004); Linda Babcock and Sara Laschever, *Ask for It: How Women Can Use the Power of Negotiation to Get What They Really Want* (Bantam, 2008).

"People will do something only if it can be demonstrated that doing so is in their best interests as defined by their own values."[73]

In other words, What's In It For Them (WIIFT) to negotiate on your issue? Link your ask to the other party's stated needs and missions. How might it serve them to agree to your asks? The more accurately you can guess the other party's assumptions and intentions, the better you can target the intersection between their needs and yours and identify what will probably be the major differences to be bridged.

Then, to the extent you can, practice adapting your approach to what the other party might find most persuasive: Big picture thinking, or detailed analyses, or both? Quantitative data, or examples and stories? Enthusiastic, or measured and calm presentations? If you're unsure, use variety.

Preparation also includes deciding on a Best Alternative to a Negotiated Agreement (BATNA). If reaching an agreement isn't possible, have a dignified closing phrase handy. Some examples: "Thanks for meeting to discuss this." "I'll assume the door is open for a reconsideration at some point." "I'm willing to accept the status quo/delay for now, but I hope we can come to a better agreement."

Role-playing the negotiation with a trusted colleague who can play devil's advocate further readies you. That's how you discover where you're weak and can try out different tactics and levels of intensity and formality, and how to make your most important points stand out. Ask your practice partner to lob at you the most crushing thing your counterpart might say. Hard-driving negotiators know how to make others uncomfortable. Practice responding until you feel strong.

---

73. Marshall Goldsmith, *Mojo: How to Get It, How to Keep It, How to Get It Back if You Lose It* (Hyperion, 2009).

Arrive with a relational opening: "How have you been? ... I've been looking forward to learning more about the possibilities for X." Prepare a few general comments or questions that might serve as a bridge: "Has any new information come to light since we last spoke?" Then offer a brief outline of your goals for the discussion.

The final preparation occurs in the interval immediately prior to the exchange. If necessary, psych yourself up with push-ups, a brisk walk, or music. Alternatively, calm yourself with slow, deep breathing, perhaps while lying on the floor and relaxing into the earth. Finally, take "superhero stance" for a few minutes, planting your feet hips-width apart, breathing from the diaphragm, and activating your personal power center and, it's been shown, a release of testosterone.

Remember: You're bringing something of great value to the table that the other party needs, or you wouldn't be at the table.

Information Exchange and Bargaining

Ascertaining *what is actually negotiable* is often the hardest challenge, especially during job-related negotiations. Depending on the industry, there may be many possibilities besides salary, including signing bonus, support for professional development, options regarding noncompete clauses, and flexible work arrangements. Prepare by quizzing friends and colleagues who are one or two steps ahead of you about their experience in this regard.

Sometimes the straightforward question, "What aspects of this are negotiable?" will suffice, although the answer will be only partially true. A rule of management is to never give anything away. Financial cards are held especially close to the vest. It's better to seek too much than too little. Bosses initially offer less than they are willing to pay; if they want you, there's always wiggle room.

To uncover relevant information that's not volunteered, arrive with probes that are open-ended and reality-testing (Chapter 6). Good questions invite the other to reveal more than what is first offered and can surface agendas. They can also demonstrate to the other party that you're working with them to find solutions. Good questions at the right time can also slow things down when needed.

Test for understanding, if necessary, repeating key words used by the other party ("Do I understand you to mean ...?"). Avoid the word *but*—it sounds as if you're contradicting the other party. *At the same time* is more helpful: *both* your truth *and* theirs are relevant.

Once you have conveyed your main message, pause; be quiet. Silences may literally be golden. Don't negotiate against yourself by filling a pause. If silence doesn't come naturally, practice fifteen seconds with a relaxed expression on your face (use a mirror or video yourself). Silences or the word "no" can have many meanings: "I'm not ready to agree"; "You're making me uncomfortable"; "I want something else"; "I need more information before agreeing."

If it serves you, try to broaden the focus; for instance, "My people are really concerned about Y and stretched by X. Are other divisions seeing this? Why do you think that is?" Come prepared with ideas for expanding the pie, which is almost never fixed: "If I join your team, I'll strengthen it with XYZ," and, "If you can't agree to X, what about Y?"

Keep some dispassionate phrases handy; for example: "I wasn't prepared for such a negative reaction. Here's why...." "I really had more than that in mind." "I didn't realize our visions were so far apart." "That's a point to consider." "I'm sure that together we can puzzle this through."

If an agreement is reached, ask, "Who else needs to sign off on this before it's final?" Follow up with an email articulating your understanding of the agreement and requesting confirmation. For example, "Unless I hear back differently from you, I'll assume this is an accurate summary with which you concur."

If the next step is signing a legal contract, it's usually a good idea to review it with a lawyer who can help you understand the implications of what you're signing.

If an agreement is not reached, debrief by writing notes about what you observed and learned. Review this with your practice partner or other experienced colleague. Don't allow your inner critic to flood you with loser messages. Even when outcomes are suboptimal, confident self-advocacy and educated bargaining efforts gain others' respect and ultimately pay off. And, if you're simultaneously building relationships, it's usually possible to renegotiate at some point.

Sample responses when Plan A is not happening:

"Please help me understand how you arrived at this conclusion."

"What other options are available to us to consider?"

"If we can't reach an agreement, let's consider what's at stake, what won't happen, and what's put at risk."

Examples of challenging statements and possible replies:

"Our tight budget can't accommodate this."

"I appreciate that you have many other demands on limited resources. At the same time, you've stated that X is a priority, and that's why what I'm asking for represents an investment you won't regret."

"You put me in a difficult position."

"That's not my intent. Let's return to what you stand to gain if we can come to an agreement."

"I'd like to pay you X, but Y won't let me."

"What would be a next step?"

"How much did you make in your last job?"

"These two situations are not comparable because of XYZ."

"Doesn't your husband make a lot?"

"That is not relevant to our discussion."

"Your husband is thriving in his job, and you wouldn't want to move your children, so you're not going anywhere, right?"

"My husband wants me to be happy, and we're discussing alternatives to our present situation."

If asked something that is illegal:

"My professional qualifications are clear, and that's what we're here to discuss."

If offered less of a package than is required by the job demands:

"That's only half of the resources we need to accomplish what I've outlined. Let's go back to the scope of work and see what to cut."

If overdue for a raise:

"How are we going to get my salary up to the mean, even though, as you know, I've never done a day of just average-level work?"

"It's time we talked about a raise and a promotion, right? Here's why I'm bringing this up now and what I propose. When can we discuss this face-to-face?"

"Perhaps my commitment to this work has misled you. I'm no longer willing to keep at this without the necessary resources."

If met with a blank stare and a noncommittal response, "I don't remember promising that"; or, "We can't agree to that"; or, "That's not our policy":

"I thought we had an informal agreement that, in exchange for X, I would be a front-runner for Y and be eligible for Z. What has changed?"

"Could you please say a little more about that or give me an example?" (Getting them talking may reveal an opening.)

The Gender Pay Gap

Many women are so used to doing whatever is asked that they miss their best opportunities to get what they need in return. On top of that, attempting to negotiate during a job interview tends to hurt women's, but not men's, chances of being hired.[74] While men are expected to be upfront about their financial needs, because women may be punished for mentioning them, they too often just accept the first offer ("Sounds great, I'll take it!"). Some women purposely don't press on salary because they require more flexibility than those without so many family responsibilities.

---

74. Linda Babcock and Sara Laschever, *Women Don't Ask: Negotiation and the Gender Divide* (Bantam, 2011).

Women compound these disadvantages if they:

▶ Wait to be noticed rather than drawing attention to their strengths (Chapter 1).

▶ Assume that it's necessary to meet 100% of the criteria before applying for a position. (Men tend to believe they're qualified if they meet about 60% of the criteria.)

▶ Talk too much—jumping the net and returning their own serves.

▶ Avoid risks and conflict.

▶ Fear the word *no*.

▶ Defer to bullies.

▶ Expect others to share their values.

▶ Are too rule oriented. (There is usually wiggle room; how much depends on who's asking.)

▶ Assume raises are rewards for past contributions, whereas bosses think of raises as investments in future performance.

▶ Agree to things in the hall (otherwise known as "ambush negotiations").

Most of these difficulties are symptoms of deeper system issues (Appendix 1). Decades of studies show that gender-linked salary discrepancies self-perpetuate and require concerted efforts to correct.[75] Journalist Sally Jenkins has written about the US champion women's soccer team's sustained and finally victorious push to win compensation equity, commenting that "money is respect."

Those who don't represent their own interests lose a lot. A large study published in *Health Affairs* found that women physicians earn

---

75. Amy S. Gottlieb, *Closing the Gender Pay Gap in Medicine: A Roadmap for Healthcare Organizations and the Women Physicians Who Work for Them* (Springer, 2020).

$2 million less than men over the course of their careers.[76] Moreover, unequal pay is so demoralizing that it contributes to burnout as well as to financial insecurity.

Individual women can't wait for their institutions to make corrections. They must take the initiative at the negotiating table, or lose out. Some women find strength in acting as if they are negotiating on behalf of a deserving friend or their whole team. While the necessary game-playing may feel as comfortable as a root canal, representing your interests as effectively as you can is empowering.

Questions for Reflection

- ▶ What have you learned from unsuccessful negotiations?
- ▶ What aspects of negotiation have you gotten better at with practice?
- ▶ What do you need to negotiate for, or to renegotiate? To connect your issues to the other party's, how will you generate a WIIFT?
- ▶ In your experience, what disadvantages do women tend to face in negotiating?

---

76. The New York Times, https://www.nytimes.com/2021/12/06/health/women-doctors-salary-pay-gap.html.

CHAPTER 9

INCREASE CAPACITIES FOR COMPLEXITY AND ORGANIZATIONAL POLITICS

Being right is interesting, but it's often irrelevant.
—Kathleen Reardon

The greater the emerging complexity,
the less we can rely on past experience.
—Otto Scharmer

▶ *Pay attention to how things get done within your organization.*

▶ *Seek out colleagues who can help you learn from your surprises and disappointments.*

▶ *Take on tasks that push you to grow in pace with the complexities you face.*

Capacity for Complexity

Constructive influence depends upon capacity for complexity. Although we tend to conflate the terms *complicated* and *complex*, differentiating between them is instructive. A good example of a complicated system is building a rocket: protocols and formulas guide the work, exact relationships among parts are specified, and one success increases the likelihood of another.[77]

But the challenges of rocket science pale in comparison to complex challenges such as raising a child or merging two hospital systems. Protocols have limited applicability. Each child, each hospital, is unique, so there are no guarantees of success, and parts cannot be separated from the whole. With dynamic complexities, cause and effect are distant in space and time, so the relationships among critical variables take a long time to tease out.[78]

Academic health systems in the US are good examples of complex organizations. They feature multiple competing missions (patient care, community service, education, and research) with key stakeholders holding conflicting views of these missions. Even without factoring in pandemics, disruptive changes and fresh sources of competition are becoming more common in all industries. Holding a leadership role in a complex organization can feel like playing high-speed, three-dimensional chess.

Questions for Reflection

▶ What in your life has gone from being complicated to complex? Anything in the reverse direction?

▶ What insights do you gain when you differentiate between your complicated challenges and those that are complex?

---

77. Brenda Zimmerman, Michael Patton, and Frances Westley, *Getting to Maybe: How the World Is Changed* (Random House, 2006).

78. Alexander Grashow, Marty Linsky, and Ronald Heifetz, *The Practice of Adaptive Leadership: Tools and Tactics for Changing Your Organization and the World* (Harvard Business School Press, 2009).

Optimal Challenges

How do we keep adapting to the multidimensional complexity that surrounds us? Educators Robert Kegan and Lisa Lahey teach that the capacity for complexity is closely linked to the abilities to question our beliefs, synthesize the perspectives of others, and appreciate that change is the natural order of life.[79]

These abilities are central to holding more than one interpretation of an event so that we may consider multiple ways of connecting the dots. As we notice more, our databases grow. To incubate these abilities, Kegan and Lahey teach that we require "optimal challenges": "the persistent experience of some frustration or quandary that is perfectly designed to cause us to feel the limits of our current way of knowing, with sufficient support so that we are neither overwhelmed by nor able to escape the conflict"[80] (see also Chapter 11).

Questions for Reflection

▶ What optimal challenges have you faced? How have these experiences increased your ability to handle additional complexities?

Competing Commitments

If our identity has become attached to an outcome, if we are dependent on any person or fused with any need, by definition, we are too close to these needs to see them fully. Objectivity is always elusive

---

79. Robert Kegan and Lisa Laskow Lahey, *Immunity to Change: How to Overcome It and Unlock the Potential in Yourself and Your Organization* (Harvard Business School Press, 2009).
80. Kegan and Lahey, *Immunity to Change*.

(Chapter 5). Any distance or elevation we achieve enables a bit more clarity about our attachments and commitments.

How do we get better at having our commitments rather than our commitments having us?

Kegan and Lahey recommend an exercise where we first articulate *our most genuine commitments*. Next, we note *which commitments are competing*—that is, preventing a change in a direction we espouse. We've often got one foot on the brake and the other on the gas. For example, I may say I'm committed to fully engaging my team, but at the same time, I'm unwilling to give up control. Kegan and Lahey next advise that I look at *what fears are holding this conflict in place*. I see my fear-driven assumptions that if I share key responsibilities, things will go downhill and my power will diminish. This exercise helps us see where we're stuck and the sources of our ambivalence.

Ambivalence is normal. Many of our processing systems operate in parallel, so we are often pushed/pulled in two directions at once; for example, simultaneously experiencing desire and fear, enthusiasm and hesitation. As discussed in Chapter 3, acknowledging our ambivalence reveals what values we're negotiating between, equipping us to evaluate our options.

Questions for Reflection

▶ Do you have any commitments that are competing where you've got one foot on the brake and the other on the gas?

▶ What are you ambivalent about? What is this teaching you?

Develop Organizational Savvy

"The grass is always greener over the septic tank," said humorist Erma Bombeck, possibly referring to organizational politics.

During the seventy-plus years of the battle for women's suffrage in the US, among the dozens of reasons put forward for denying women the vote was protecting them from the "filth" and "depravity" of politics.[81]

Poli (many) + ticks (blood-sucking bugs) is actually how most of my clients feel about politics; many are pierced by dismay at the political maneuverings that affect them. But the word *politics* shares the same root as *people*. Wherever we find people, we find competition for resources and power. The more complex the hierarchies, the more complex the politics, and the more success depends on what the culture defines as important.

A lack of attention to the exercise of power within organizations ensures a lack of influence. An organizational chart, which shows only the major reporting relationships, cannot offer many clues about how things get done. Each organization has its own nervous system of shifting connections and influence, along with vulnerabilities in its operating system. Learning how to get things done with the least amount of conflict occurs only gradually and only as you take on more responsibilities and gain exposure to how your role and unit fit into the larger picture.

Clarity will be fleeting, however. As organizational performance expert Karl Weick teaches, in most organizations, discrepancies are common between what is espoused and what is actually done. Sense occurs only in "small bursts."[82] We endeavor to "access our ignorance"; that is, to locate what we don't understand and then formulate questions that will reduce our ignorance.[83]

---

81. Elaine Weiss, *The Woman's Hour: The Great Fight to Win the Vote* (Penguin, 2018).

82. Karl Weick, *Making Sense of the Organization* (Wiley Blackwell, 2000).

83. Edgar Schein, *Humble Consulting: How to Provide Real Help Faster* (Berrett-Koehler, 2016).

Arriving at useful interpretations of events that affect us depends on relationships with those who can see more of the picture than we can and who can extend our understanding of what constraints are emerging, how decisions are made, and which situations we can influence. We keep trying to connect with "connectors"— those who already have rich networks and readily link up others with common interests. Developing such linkages takes effort and relational savvy. Key here is the ability to make good use of every opportunity to bridge to and dialogue with colleagues about what's important to both of you, and to respect boundaries so as not to wear out your welcome.

Cultures where members are encouraged to make their observations available to others are the strongest. Management consultant Nancy Dixon recommends that organizations create "hallways"[84] where members make their interpretations accessible to others, where the data on which conclusions are based can be challenged and the reasoning that led to the conclusions examined.

In isolation we tend to arrive at unfounded assumptions. For instance, a physician directing a clinic in an underserved area assumes that the clinic is "untouchable," because it is central to the medical center's mission. She subsequently misses chances to influence the CFO who is working to shut the clinic down. In retrospect, she sees that her dedication interfered with staying on top of the financials and recruiting well-placed allies of the clinic.

Getting sidetracked by how things *should be* interferes with analysis of what *is*. Righteous indignation frequently gets in the way of the wise use of our influence. And the work of distinguishing between

---

84. Nancy Dixon, "Where Is the Only Place Employees Share Their Knowledge? The Hallways of Learning," *Conversation Matters*, April 1, 2022, https://www.nancydixonblog.com/2022/04/where-is-the-only-place-employees-share-their-knowledge.html.

what we can and cannot influence is continuous. Feelings of agitation and frustration are usually clues that our assumptions are in error; we seek out colleagues who can help us think more analytically.

Questions for Reflection

▶ How would you rate your networking skills and opportunities? What actions might you take to expand your circle of trusted colleagues?

▶ What issues within your department/organization do you need to better understand? Who might help you?

▶ What disadvantages have you noticed that women and people of color face in getting things done within your organization?

▶ How do you interpret this equation from a Harvard Business Review blog: "Success = (Purpose x Talent) to the power of Culture"?

Trust

Especially when we're new in an organization, it's hard to know who we can trust. In deciding whether someone is trustworthy, people tend to overrely on reputation, apparent confidence, how similar they are to the other person, and on how much they think they need the person's help. In the absence of facts, we tend to assemble either self-serving or paranoid narratives. Skepticism can be a virtue here, especially if we tend to put those we admire on a pedestal.

Trust is not an either/or phenomenon. Since we can rarely afford to just write someone off, we consider how trustworthiness depends on *context*. We remain alert to situations in which someone's competence or integrity is thrown into question and to when their judgments seem sound, and revise our expectations accordingly. The shift to remote work has made these observations trickier.

Everyone endures disappointments, if not worse, when it comes to over-trusting the wrong person. I was devastatingly wrong about a longtime colleague and friend whose career I'd aided and who had served as a resource in my work. Overlooking that we would be competing for the same business, I naively took her advice on something that ended up delaying my success.

My error in judgment arose from conflating unconditional relationships with conditional relationships. Unconditional relationships, such as those with a loving family, can thrive independent of contexts. By contrast, all professional relationships are conditional, dependent on roles which at some point shift; for example, a friend becomes a direct report, a boss, or a competitor. I came to see how common this conflation is among women who unconsciously expect women professionals to be more relational than men are (Appendix 1).

Agility requires analysis of our relational disappointments. We offer our confusion a chair and see what can be learned: How were my expectations out of line? What clues did I miss? What assumptions were blinding me and why? What attachments were interfering with my objectivity? What values are involved? Who might help me dissect this? Do I need to go to therapy? Once we've extracted what intelligence we can, we let go of the disappointment.

Questions for Reflection

▶ If your trust in someone important to you has ever been misplaced, what of continuing value did you learn from what happened and your role in it?

▷ From analyzing relational disappointments, what patterns have you noticed? What do these reveal about your habits, strengths, temperament, defenses, perceptual filters?

Finite and Infinite Games

All politics can be considered "finite games."[85] Finite games are played for the sake of ending them (for example, a tennis match, hiring an assistant). "Infinite games" are played for the sake of playing and of growing, especially in concert with others. Contrasting finite games with infinite games often lifts me above the mire into the bigger picture.

Finite players play within boundaries (for example, lots of hierarchies and rules); anything contained within a boundary will exhaust itself. Infinite players, ever curious, play with boundaries and edges.

With finite games, only one player or team can win, although other contestants may well be ranked at the conclusion of play. Winners must prove repeatedly that they are winners. Finite players are usually quite serious about competing, even though the abstractions they are playing for (power, money, titles) are worthless unless they are visible to others.

Infinite players regard their wins and losses as moments in continuing play. They are not limited by zero-sum assumptions and are always alert to possibilities for "expanding the pie" (Chapter 5).

I recently received delightful evidence of my continuing shift to infinite play. A colleague nominated me for a national award, and two other very highly regarded colleagues gladly wrote letters on my behalf affirming my accomplishments in ways so meaningful to me that I don't care whether I win the finite game of the award competition.

---

85. James Carse, *Finite and Infinite Games: A Vision of Life as Play and Possibility* (Ballantine Books, 1986).

When the Border Isn't Clear

Subject as we are to financial pressures and competing commitments, maintaining an infinite mindset is not easy.[86] Our physiology also complicates discernment. Winning a competition rewards the brain with a lovely hit of dopamine. Sports are fun! Also, getting credit or seeing our name in print is so satisfying.

Not all commitments divide neatly into finite or infinite. For instance, one of my clients built an internationally respected program boosting primary care education and research, only to have the dean snatch it up to sweeten the package to recruit a "big name" (giving it to the guy's wife, no less). Naturally for a while, this felt like career death, but she rallied and has thrived. Similarly, an artist's failed search for an agent when she has put a decade into a book may feel infinitely discouraging.

When faced with a major disappointment, if we can take the long view, gaining some distance and/or higher ground, we will see fresh possibilities in what once felt like a total loss. But sometimes we have to make a major change. If we lose trust in the leaders of our organization or conclude that the culture no longer aligns with our goals, it is usually less risky to leave than to stay. If circumstances demand that we stay, clarity about our motives facilitates our acceptance of the trade-offs and sacrifices.

While finding a more conducive environment or starting one's own business is not easy, agile individuals discover options. Transitions are hard. But once we're on the other side of the chaos, our horizons almost always expand in growth-promoting ways. More will be revealed, usually via our questions (Chapter 10).

---

86. Simon Sinek, *The Infinite Game* (Portfolio Penguin, 2019).

Questions for Reflection

▶ Describe a finite game that is currently gnawing at you. Try reframing it as an interval in infinite play.

▶ With a finite game that you lost, what has helped you put it in perspective? Could you have done anything to speed up this learning, or did it just take time?

PART 3

FOCUSING OVER THE LONG HAUL

PART 3: FOCUSING OVER THE LONG HAUL

CHAPTER 10

BUILD RESILIENCE

We need to think of ourselves as those who are
being questioned by life .... Life means taking the
responsibility to fulfill the tasks which it
constantly sets for each individual.
—Viktor Frankl

When the winds of change blow,
some build walls, others build windmills.
—Chinese Proverb

▶ *Be the best steward of your attention that you can be.*
▶ *Get comfortable with the discomforts of uncertainty.*
▶ *Your whys help keep you wise; mine your questions as your guide.*
▶ *Protect time off from relational responsibilities.*

I take resilience to mean resourcefulness, hardiness, and agility over
the long haul, graced with a sense of gratitude for life's gifts and with
the ability to laugh at ourselves. The concept of resilience remains
theoretical until we are tested, commonly through tragedy, or family

or personal challenges. With continual changes to adapt to and silver linings in short supply, whatever we can do to build our resilience pays off.

It's easy to name characteristics of resourceful people. They attend to their physical health and mental and emotional well-being, seeking help as needed; learn from their disappointments and mistakes; limit indulgence in nostalgia, cynicism, and righteous indignation; take smart risks in the service of their values; and build a supportive community. This chapter offers reflections on how we can build these capacities over a lifetime.

Abraham Maslow's concept of a hierarchy of needs offers reminders about the basics. First are physiological needs for nutrition and sleep. Next are needs for safety and shelter. Once these are met, we become aware of the social needs of inclusion and a sense of belonging. Feelings of self-esteem and of competence then become possible. For those born into privilege, it's easy to forget that billions of people live with many of these needs unmet.

What Influences the Building of Resilience?

Many conditions interact to influence how people respond to and learn from stressful experiences and whether these build or detract from their resilience. Even good health and access to nutritious food, safe housing, and a stable home life don't guarantee resilience. Common challenges include:

▶ *Inhumane systems and workplaces*: Dehumanizing jobs and contentious environments can diminish our access to our strengths so much that we may even blame ourselves for how erased or reduced we feel. We take care of ourselves as best we can until we can relocate into a better fit.

▶ *The tyranny of the urgent*: If we're putting out fires every day, the goals closest to our heart remain unreachable. "When you're pressed for time, infinity may as well not be there," says Lily Tomlin. We might ask ourselves: "What can I put less of myself into so that I have more energy for what's more important over the long haul?"

▶ *Resisting the inevitability of loss*: We *suffer* loss, and there's no immunity. When a loved one, a job, or a wallet crosses the line separating what was once central to our lives from what is no longer, we grieve for as long as it takes. We try to cooperate, to let go of what life is taking away. Yet between the death of an old reality and the formation of a new one, there is often a period of chaos that we can't think our way out of. As we accept the inescapability of this temporary zone of confusion, creative new possibilities often open.[87]

▶ *Ruminating on past events and holding on to stories and events that no longer serve us*: Author Lewis Hyde writes that memory functions best in tandem with forgetting.[88] Forgetting—when not a symptom of illness—is necessary for storing what deserves to be preserved and for remaining present-centered. Rather than letting a dreadful memory unspool freely in vivid detail yet again, we can switch gears the instant we notice it. We have more power than we imagine to prevent our minds from causing us more suffering.

▶ *Comparing ourselves to others*: Achieving escape velocity from internally- and culturally-generated constrictions depends on staying rooted in our own strengths and accept-

---

87. William Bridges, *The Way of Transition: Embracing Life's Most Difficult Moments* (Perseus Books Group, 2001).

88. Lewis Hyde, *A Primer for Forgetting: Getting Past the Past* (Farrar, Straus & Giroux, 2019).

ing our eccentricities. But in comparing ourselves to the limited information we have about others, we shortchange our own values and experiences. We are in essence robbing from ourselves.

▶ *Expecting others to share our values:* If our strongest value is, say, responsibility or generosity, and we expect others to live up to our particular standards of this trait, we will be frequently disappointed. Adapting our expectations does not indicate a lowering of standards. We are broadening our ability to relate to others, becoming more versatile.

▶ *Concluding that we are insignificant:* When we feel inept or fragile, we may feel like giving up, as if our actions don't matter. These feelings signal that it's time to turn to someone who can help us to see the bigger reality of our gifts and options. Also, paradoxically serving someone else, even in a small way, deepens our feeling of connection to our own humanity.

Questions for Reflection

▶ Which of these challenges do you feel are interfering with your resilience? Alternatively, which are serving to build your resilience as you adapt to the difficulties?

The Wise Use of Attention

Resilience requires us to manage how we focus our precious and always limited attention. What gains our attention shapes us. Author David Foster Wallace famously said: "If you cannot or will not choose what you pay attention to and choose how you construct meaning from experience, you will be totally hosed."

As daily life floods us with interruptions, distractions, stomach-churning news, and frustrating choices, how can we not feel hosed? Too much information—and now disinformation; i.e., lies—equates to a poverty of attention. We want to be good shepherds of our attention, but the sheep go astray. In taking responsibility for this shepherding, it's important to occasionally assess our media-related choices. Likewise, we update our systems for capturing the information we need and for deleting what we don't.

Every day we work at maintaining an analytic focus on what we can influence and letting go of what we can't. How much of our bandwidth is spent regretting the past or arguing with people who are not in the room? Our useless ruminations usually nag on recurring subjects; writing stream-of-consciousnessly on those subjects can reveal patterns.

Reflecting on the following questions may also help give repetitive thoughts the boot:

▶ What are my contributions to what I complain about?

▶ Who no longer deserves rent-free space in my head? My heart?

▶ What is my worrying trying to protect me from?

▶ When I get defensive, what am I usually trying to protect?

Another dimension of how we use our attention relates to the tight connection between moving and thinking, an evolutionary legacy. Author Annie Murphy Paul summarized many recent studies showing how the physical state we're in when we encounter information dramatically affects the way we process it.[89] For instance, moving sharpens our visual sense, and brisk exercise readies us to learn something new. When our frazzled attention requires resto-

---

89. Annie Murphy Paul, *The Extended Mind: The Power of Thinking Outside the Brain* (Mariner Books, 2021).

ration, a walk in a park is especially rejuvenating. Natural scenes offer redundant and predictable information. Gazing at fractals—for instance, tree branchings, gaps in tree canopies, ferns, ocean waves—supports feeling at ease and wakefully relaxed. This natural fluidity feels excellent and healthy.

The capacity to shift our focus back into the here and now also improves with mindfulness and meditation practices. Even something as simple as stretching or counting breaths can be restorative. As we develop a more open and positive focus, our maps of the world grow richer, and we get smarter. And when our troubles are obscuring our gifts, reminding ourselves of all the tough stuff we have already survived and naming what we're grateful for today can be empowering.

Questions for Reflection

▶ What are you learning about improving your focus on what's most important?

▶ What repetitive thoughts tend to plague you? What is the story with these?

▶ Have you found this statement by Daniel Kahneman to be true: "Nothing in life is as important as you think it is while you're thinking about it"?

Comfort with the Discomforts of Uncertainty

Prophets, dictators, oracles, and evangelical preachers have always been popular among humans seeking to escape the tortures of uncertainty. Since the brain is constantly trying to predict the near future, uncertainty generates an error response, like a flashing light. Distress alerts us to danger. A lack of control can feel physically uncomfortable, because drops in the opioid level in our brain put us into a mild state of narcotic withdrawal.[90]

We can't help wishing for more stability than is ever available. Wars, global warming and pandemics only heighten these longings. To all our shared uncertainties, we each add our own private, destabilizing doubts. Since uncertainty is inevitable, and it's human nature to be unsettled by discomfort, we are left with an oxymoron: *How do we become more comfortable with the discomforts of uncertainty?*

As we stop resisting the messiness of life, we wear our ups and downs more like a loose garment and less like cling wrap. We hold our tensions a bit more lightly, with less wear and tear on our minds and bodies. As our comfort zones expand, we become more creative in modifying our expectations and adapting to the losses attendant upon maturing and aging in our chaotic world.

Questions for Reflection

▶ How might you deepen your comfort with the discomforts of uncertainty?

▶ What are you resisting that it would serve you to try to welcome?

The Discipline of Reflection

Reflecting on what holds great meaning for us strengthens our ability to weather our challenges. Jung advised: "If we fail to engage in cogent dialogue with the questions that emerge from our depths, we live unconsciously, accidentally." The quests in our questions reflect our fears, aspirations, and sources of ambivalence. Going toward, rather than shying

---

90. Suchman, "Uncertainty," 554–555.

away from, thorny questions expands our acceptance of "uncertainties, mysteries, doubts," as the poet John Keats framed this capacity.

Some commit to an annual reflection practice in conjunction with a birthday or new year. Others link this discipline to an annual performance review, during which they set personal learning goals in addition to job-related ones. Whether part of a regular practice or not, I recommend stream-of-consciousness writing on whatever is front and center that can be sorted later into categories and mined for themes deserving of contemplation.

I also suggest taking notes in response to whichever of the following questions hit home. Retaining these interior sketches over a number of years can provide a unique source of insight into our own development, revealing as nothing else can: how our conceptual language is expanding; what assumptions and labels are interfering with our learning; what we could give ourselves more credit for; where we are wrong; where we can lighten up on ourselves; and where we are stuck.

Questions for Reflection

▶ What do you understand or have a fresh perspective on now that you didn't a year ago? What prepared you for this insight?

▶ What is the biggest risk you've taken? What did you learn from it?

▶ What were your biggest surprises? What assumptions does this reveal? What clues did you miss because of your temperament? Your perceptual filters? Strong preferences? Blind spots?

▶ What are you ambivalent about? What is this ambivalence helping you see?

▶ Is your professional identity linked to, or dependent on, something you'll never be good at or enjoy? If so, can you delegate this? What else might you try?

▶ What are you gripping that you might hold a bit more lightly?

▶ To whom have you given unearned power?

▶ What are you taking for granted that you could more consciously appreciate? What's a first step?

▶ What are you developing gratitude for that you once took for granted? Who deserves your thanks and how will you express it?

▶ What are your sources of wealth?

▶ What would it take to develop more of a sense of humor about your flaws and blind spots, to be able to laugh at yourself more often?

▶ If you were writing or filming the story of your life, what might be the first sentence or sequence?

Protect Time Free of Relational Responsibilities

Remaining open and curious takes energy. In the rush of the work week (which now lasts seven days for many), serious introspection is rarely possible. Protecting, as best we can, intervals where our minds can drift and wander free of routine and responsibilities improves our abilities to organize ourselves, to innovate, and to make long-term decisions.[91]

The often-touted concept of "balance" oversimplifies our lived realities. A balance implies two elements that can be kept in correct proportion—in effect, pitting them against each other. David Whyte instead offers the image of three "marriages,"[92] or primary categories of relationships, we form in life: with our work, with multiple significant others, and with ourselves. These are not separate commitments but different expressions of how we belong in the world. Keeping our

---

91. Johann Hari, *Stolen Focus: Why You Can't Pay Attention—and How to Think Deeply Again* (Crown, 2022).

92. David Whyte, *The Three Marriages: Reimagining Work, Self and Relationship* (Riverhead Books, 2010).

commitments in conversation with each other encourages insights into the tensions we experience.

Of course, our commitments often compete for our best energies, and the relationship that gets shortchanged is usually the one with ourselves. Many assume that protecting time and space for ourselves will be considered selfish. It can take courage to close the door, block out the time, turn off the phone. But even brief intervals free of relational responsibilities can pay dividends. High-quality solitude expands our bandwidth and reveals creative solutions to everyday problems, inaugurating a friendlier view of ourselves and our world. (See more suggestions in the section Give Yourself Restorative Breaks.).

Questions for Reflection

▶ What questions central to your resilience deserve more of your attention?

▶ What's your experience with the truth of this saying by Herodotus: "If a man never allowed himself a bit of fun and relaxation, he would become unstable without knowing it"?

▶ How might you apply poet Rilke's famous advice to "Be patient toward all that is unsolved in your heart and try to love the questions themselves"?

Resilience as a Team and Community Member

Taking on tasks that are larger than us that add value to humankind requires even sturdier levels of resilience because of the often massive inconveniences of working with others. Strong teamwork and group facilitation skills are things of beauty requiring years of practice with the elements discussed in Chapters 4-9. Two aspects deserve particular emphasis:

First, thinking within groups asks us to make our logic visible so that others can follow us. If we supply unnecessary details or over-elaborate, people lose patience or tune out. We strive to supply just enough relevant background.

Second is the work of helping a group to expand their pie of options and to maximize the upsides of their polarities. This depends on our recognizing the traps of false dichotomies and either/or thinking (Chapter 5).

Contributing anything of importance over the long haul requires perseverance and courage. I've gleaned supportive reminders from the work of Meg Wheatley.[93] When we find ourselves asking, "Why am I doing all this hard work?" one answer may be, "Because it is my turn to serve the world out of my strengths in this way at this juncture." At the same time we give up every shred of the idea that if we just worked harder, we could accomplish more. And we take the long view, letting go of needing our service to change the world now.

Eckhart Tolle also encourages us to, "Accept—then act. Whatever the present moment contains, accept it as if you had chosen it. Always work with it, not against it."

Questions for Reflection

▶ What skills do you need to hone to improve your contributions to a group that's important to you?

▶ What groups should you consider dropping out of?

---

93. Wheatley, *Perseverance*.

Give Yourself Restorative Breaks

There's no formula for the renewal of our minds and spirit. Each culture evolves its own approaches, and each person has her own preferences. The goal is to create conditions for setting down our weighty backpack of agendas and responsibilities. High-quality relaxation combined with high-quality introspection opens us to what life most wants to teach us about what really matters and reduces the pressures we experience to conform.

I consider these breaks to be an "advance" rather than a "retreat." A spacious inner stillness is both a major achievement and a boon allowing us to become better custodians of our minds and more astute students of the universe.

I find that even one day and night in an environment conducive to reflection and rejuvenation can be extremely valuable—whether in a retreat center, a place with woods for walking in, an Airbnb near water, or even a nice hotel. In solitude and silence, the energy I usually invest in others stays focused inside where it has a chance to distill into self-knowledge and self-compassion. During longer protected intervals, unimagined changes in perspective and capacities have evolved.

Each person will have her own way of making the most of protected time. I've found the following practices of value:

▶ Limiting input (food, music, reading, and of course screen time).

▶ Taking care of the body's needs for both movement and relaxation. (Yoga helps, as we remember that yoga means a "yoking" of body, mind, and spirit.)

▶ Setting the goal of staying present in the here and now. We repeatedly use the breath to bring the mind home to the body and the body home to the mind. This goal may feel out of reach or uncomfortably boring, especially if we are accustomed to constant mental or physical movement. But as we settle down, we discover moments of stillness when our true nature of basic goodness may reveal itself.

▶ Arriving with a few questions for reflection. For example: "What have been the significant stepping stones (events) and crossroads (choices) in my life? What do I appreciate about these now that I couldn't when they occurred? What is essential to my happiness now, and why?" We nonjudgmentally note whatever thoughts, emotions, or sensations arise, honoring any regrets or uncertainties as teachers. If the introspection goes south and the going gets tough, we turn to wonder, as in, "I wonder what triggered that reaction? What started me off on that tangent?" If feelings of panic or confusion arise, we greet them, "Hello, my restlessness. We will be okay."[94]

Access the Wisdom of Your Own Inner Teacher: An Exercise

This exercise enhances resilience by facilitating access to your own wisdom. The idea is to open to what your more experienced self might communicate to your present less secure self.

Visualize meeting up with the wiser self that will be you in twenty years (or whatever age seems good). This elder version of you is waiting for you to arrive in the beautiful space where she resides (fill this setting out in your imagination). She hugs you in greeting, welcoming you just as you are. She invites you to open your heart.

---

94. As Thich Nhat Hanh often recommended.

What do you need from her? You may bring general or specific questions or fears. For instance, "Since you understand a great deal more than I do about what really matters, what advice or reassurances do you have for me? What do you know now that you wish you had known at my age?" You may receive a phrase or a wordless feeling of enduring and comforting significance to you. Take notes.

CHAPTER 11

CHART YOUR OWN COURSE

How singular each of us is in the way we hold a conversation
with life—a particular way of shaping ourselves in the world.
—David Whyte

To have courage for whatever comes in life—
everything lies in that.
—Teresa of Avila

Life is short, and the arts of human inner and relational growth are
long. In this closing chapter, let's review what seems central to our
continuing unfolding.

When many priorities are competing for attention, ask: "*Why* am
I doing what I'm doing? What are my goals and motives? What do I
need to let go of? Why am I putting so much pressure on myself?"
Freedom lies in controlling how much energy we put into anything.

Stay open to what's emerging. There is a "cure" in curiosity.

Give the body what it needs to thrive, accepting its limitations as
gracefully as possible.

Pause more often to recenter. Slowing down encourages savoring
the joys and pleasures any day may offer—for instance, noticing how

the sun and rain-filled clouds are present in our bread.[95] During a present-centered pause, check in with your emotional and physical pulses and stretch what's tight. When we're tuned in to these often subtle clues, we notice what's contracting us and instinctively adopt a more expansive attitude.

Build in unstructured breaks from routine and relational responsibilities so that the mind can play and wander. In particular, time outdoors where the eye meets no walls puts the human brain at ease and encourages fresh ideas and improved mood.

Stay in touch with friends with whom you can fully relax into your vulnerable, inquiring, and eccentric self. At the same time, look for opportunities to expand connections and learn from those with whom you have less in common.

Rather than trying to get better at what you'll never be good at, buy what assistance you can, and learn how to delegate.

Know when and how to ask for help. When we're processing something terrifying, depressing, or puzzling, sharing almost always halves our darkness. Know when to be specific, for example: "Please just listen." "Tell me how this comes across to you." "I welcome any feedback on X." As we more readily and wisely open these relational doors, not only do we reduce the isolating illusion that we're supposed to be able to figure everything out by ourselves, but we also affirm the unique value of each relationship. Likewise, as opportunities arise, we look for ways to support and affirm each other's bravery.

Allow to fall away what doesn't serve, especially painful memories and resentments. Forgiveness heals.

Some of these beneficial practices may come naturally, but they usually require patient years of personalizing and cultivating disci-

---

95. Thich Nhat Hanh, "How to Eat," *Plum Village*, September 1, 2021, https://plumvillage.app/how-to-eat/.

plines and supports. Often the teachers we need arrive just as we are ready to receive them. And, gradually, our inner coach becomes ever more reliable, accessible, and empowered.

Optimal Challenges

Finally, let's revisit the advantages accruing from engaging wholeheartedly with our toughest challenges. To keep growing in pace with the complexities of our responsibilities, we require tasks that reveal our limitations but that we manage to handle. These are "optimal challenges" (Chapter 9).

The only such challenge in my life that I actually chose has been writing this book.[96] Writing about anything intensifies our engagement with it. What I've learned the most about is softening toward myself— that's what has always been hardest for me. Here are signs of my progress:

Stuck in draft zero during the initial two years of work on this book, and unable to identify my target audience or in which bookstore section any book of mine might belong, I assumed that my lonely confusion indicated that there was something wrong with me. I now see this groping as integral to my finding my focus, and I recognize that doubts and inefficiencies are natural when undertaking anything of substance.

---

96. All my other optimal challenges found me, and being ever-motivated to achieve, I plunged in headfirst. Beginning with my entry into the public school system at grade nine (after eight years of challenge-free Lutheran grade school), every subsequent year of my education presented optimal challenges. Then after six brain-deadening secretarial stints, I was in the right place at the right time to assist and learn from the students in Brown University's emerging medical school. Between 1972–1976, with virtually no guidance, I served as founding director of the admissions, financial aid, and student affairs offices. Subsequently, again in the right place at right time at the Association of American Medical Colleges (AAMC), I led and learned from the cream of the nation's crop of medical students and student affairs officers, followed by putting AAMC's Office of Women in Medicine on the national map and laying the groundwork for the Office of Faculty Affairs—again with no templates. Once I stopped growing in those roles, rather than risk stasis, I let go of security and a corner office to create my own business on the then bleeding edge of coaching physicians and scientists.

As I suffered in my initial isolation, I struggled with my friends' lack of response to my requests for feedback. Eventually, I realized that my lack of clarity about my writing goals put my friends in an impossible position. To their great credit, no one uttered an inauthentic word in response. Once I could give my friends and colleagues something solid enough to respond to, reaching out to them for feedback elicited invaluable insights and considerably deepened many of these relationships—a double blessing.

This newfound wealth has emboldened me, reminding me of the validity of my goals and values. Given the depth of my socialization-engendered self-doubt, I needed this reinforcement to persevere. This grounding has enabled me to ease up on myself and laugh more readily at my own screw-ups (I keep a red clown nose handy). My nascent sense of humor even extends to the ass-kicking craft of writing. I've progressed from being dismayed at my uncountable numbers of revisions (my drafts look like battlefields) to accepting how many ways there are to express anything complex and how long it takes for some paragraphs to come right.

This lightening and loosening up also opens me to many paradoxes of human development. I now see how once we build solid ground within ourselves, we can explore the fundamental groundlessness and interconnectedness of existence. According to David Whyte, what puts real ground under our feet is courageously dealing with our disappointments as we risk ourselves in relationships, marriage, work, life.[97] Our uncertain times demand frequent reappraisals of reality such that disappointments may be thought of as the "frontier of an evolving life."

Pema Chödrön further teaches that to really get to know our anxieties, we must refrain from the comforts of habit, from doing what

---

97. David Whyte, *Consolations: The Solace, Nourishment and Underlying Meaning of Everyday Words* (Many Rivers Press, 2014).

comes most naturally.[98] That's how we make friends with ourselves at the most profound level possible. While this is normally out of my reach, during my retreats/advances, I'm able to listen to what my restlessness is saying. A precious spaciousness may arise.

Everyone embodies a different version of taking life seriously and of connecting with what they find good. My experiences with optimal challenges convince me that unforeseeable benefits accrue when we take risks aligned with what we most value. Undertaking hard tasks seems to be how we absorb what life most wants to teach us and how we gain access to the true extent of our talents as well as to the full recognition of privileges we tend to take for granted. Finding ways to apply these gifts in service to the world is the surest way to a meaning-filled and resilient life.[99]

Sitting Beside Ourselves

Perhaps "finding our place in the firmament" more accurately represents human development than the phrase "charting our own course," which implies an unlikely degree of enduring luck, clarity, and autonomy. We do our best to make good use of whatever clarity and autonomy a given day offers without expecting ourselves to be somehow better or smarter than we are. We facilitate our progress by humbly and frequently reassessing how well our commitments, as reflected by how we use our time, reflect what we love.

The root of "reassess" means "seated beside." We companionably sit beside ourselves, giving ourselves credit for the steep climbs we've accomplished and pep talks, as needed, for the work that remains.

---

98. Chödrön, *When Things Fall Apart*.

99. George E. Vaillant, *Aging Well: Surprising Guideposts to a Happier Life from the Landmark Harvard Study of Adult Development* (Little, Brown, 2002).

This generosity toward ourselves paradoxically generates a generosity toward our fellow humans and a gratitude that reflects the highest aspirations of the human heart.

Questions for Reflection

▶ Is it time to empathically sit beside yourself and reassess a commitment or a preconception about yourself? How might such a reassessment contribute to your resilience?

▶ How would you summarize the wisdom you've accrued so far in life? What about your recurring doubts? How well do your doubts and wisdom get along?

▶ How do you interpret Annie Dillard's saying, "Our nonconformity may be our only hope"?

▶ How do you respond to Valarie Kaur's challenge, "You are alive and have something worth fighting for. How will you channel that?"

APPENDIX 1

WHAT DOES GENDER HAVE TO DO WITH CAREER DEVELOPMENT?

Women who acquire power are more likely to be criticized
for it than are the men who have always had it.
—Carolyn Heilbrun

It's your life—but only if you make it so. The standards
by which you live must be your own standards, your
own values, your own convictions in regard to ...
what is important and what is trivial.
—Eleanor Roosevelt

Most chapters of this book offer observations on challenges that women face when they get serious about translating their intellectual capital into career capital. This Appendix provides additional background on navigating these challenges.

I present a general overview of the continuing legacy of patriarchy and the masculine bias of almost everything, and then offer observations on four persistent interrelated difficulties that women tend to experience and to misinterpret as personal deficits: (1) underestimation, (2) lack of career-advancing mentoring, (3) conflating personal and professional relationships, and (4) delays in becoming a protagonist in their own lives. Understanding the common and systemic nature of these difficulties is liberating. I close with reflections on what might constitute progress in reducing gender-related inequities.

Sociocultural Heritage

All cultures facilitate the participation of some subgroups more than others. Western culture springs from the lives of educated, heterosexual, white men. Most such men remain blind to this abundant advantage—a self-deception fundamental to maintaining the status quo.[100]

The devaluation of the feminine began before recorded history. Many believe that this devaluation originated in men's fear and envy of women's capacities for giving birth and nurturing them (or withholding nurture). With the spread of agriculture in approximately 10,000 BCE, property came to be defined as "private," and a woman's body became a piece of men-controlled property.[101] With "God" defined as masculine and "the tempter" cast as feminine in many traditions, the subordination of women became divinely sanctioned as well. That all sacred texts teach deference to authority has facilitated women's acceptance of this subjugation.

It has been suggested that humans, on their way to higher civilization, had to go through a patriarchal stage of "thou shalt nots," meaning that patriarchy is less about masculinity than about law and order. And yet it seems accurate to say that patriarchy's notion of a healthy culture relies on women staying asleep to their own needs

---

100. Jessica Nordell, *The End of Bias: A Beginning: The Science and Practice of Overcoming Unconscious Bias* (Metropolitan Books, 2021).

101. Robert McElvaine, *Eve's Seed: Biology, the Sexes and the Course of History* (McGraw-Hill, 2000).

"for their own good." Even Enlightenment-era thinkers could not imagine that women's activities could extend into the public sphere or that women's time was as valuable as theirs.

Power is so deeply woven into most white men's lives that, even as they feel entitled to it, it remains invisible to them—like a wind at their back, undetectably easing their way. By contrast, any woman entering a field or room full of already well-connected men is walking into a headwind. The higher a woman climbs, the stronger the wind.

The difficulties women still face in achieving their potentials originate in this inherited culture. Assuming that these difficulties are theirs alone to solve, most women overlook how systemic and structurally rooted their challenges are.

Underestimation

My highly credentialed 29-year-old goddaughter, a first year in an international law firm, is frequently the only woman in meetings. When administrative tasks arise, the guys look first at her. She has also noticed that women professionals with a doctorate still tend to be introduced by their first name, whereas men are "Dr...." (Women in my generation have never stopped noticing this.)

Most young women also remain unprepared for the narrower band of confident behaviors they are allowed if they are to remain likeable. As one example out of hundreds, a man can raise his voice, but when a woman does, it's labeled "scolding" or "yelling," and HR gets involved. The "tone police" never sleep.[102]

Women, especially of color, also notice the "prove it again phenomenon," whereby they are repeatedly required to provide evidence of their suitability and expertise. Following a gender transition from

---

102. As observed by *The Washington Post* senior critic-at-large Robin Givhan.

male to female, more than one established scientist has discovered that she was now interrupted, ignored, and condescended to.[103]

Women who are anything less than modest about their accomplishments are considered "boastful." But advancement depends on getting credit for one's work. Male authors are more likely than women to sprinkle words like "novel," "unique," and "excellent" into the abstracts summarizing their papers. Framing findings in a positive light makes them more likely to be cited by peers, a key measure of the influence of research.

These days many forms of underestimation are so subtle, they go unnoticed except by those experiencing or studying them. For instance, even before age fifty, women evidently receive fewer callbacks during job searches than do men; men do not begin to experience age discrimination until age sixty-five. No wonder so many women start coloring their hair at the first signs of gray.

Most biases operate free of intent; that is, a man may not intend disrespect when he says, "You're too sensitive" (or "cold" or "pushy"). Women tend to complain to each other about such slights but seldom manage to constructively raise them with male friends or colleagues. Resentments ensue.

Lack of Mentoring

Another area of disadvantage for women is gaining less benefit from mentoring relationships with men than men do. Relationships form most naturally between individuals who have a lot in common and who share informal activities such as golf. Mentoring relationships also get a head start when the junior person reminds the senior person of themselves.

Men often inadvertently remain less forthcoming and patient with women protégés. Very insightful men leaders have expressed

---

103. For example: Ben A. Barres, "Does Gender Matter?" *Nature* 442 (2006): 133-137.

to me the wish that they could somehow excise the self-doubts that they notice in highly competent women protégés. But patriarchy's complex legacy disallows any such simple remedy.[104]

Possibly fearing tears, insecure men may avoid challenging their women mentees. They are thus less likely to work through difficult issues, resulting in fewer opportunities to get to know each other well. Some are using the #MeToo movement as an excuse to detach, limiting their own legacies.

Another subset of men, largely unconsciously, are comfortable relating only paternalistically to women protégés. When a woman begins spreading her wings and seeking more independence, such mentors pull away, often with no explanation. Being dropped at this critical point by the person most needed in her corner can be devastating to a woman's confidence and career. Women tend to blame themselves for this failure. Those who blame the mentor instead risk making an enemy of a powerful senior in their field.

The rare women who achieve a position of power often find that the more competent and confident they become, the lonelier they are. Isolation represents a double negative, because a rich network of colleagues is instrumental to career advancement. A sponsor and colleagues with influence are critical to gaining access to information and to opportunities.

Confusing Personal and Professional Relationships

Many women unknowingly conflate unconditional with conditional relationships. As discussed in Chapter 9, all professional relationships are conditional and dependent on roles, which at some point

---

104. Janet Bickel, "How Skilled Mentors Reduce Gender's Influence on Career and Leadership Development." *Journal of Women's Health* 31, no. 5 (2022): 609-10.

shift. If a friend becomes a boss, a direct report, or a competitor, this division between conditional and unconditional blurs. Often people's kids are on the same sports teams, partners are friends, or there are other non-job-related linkages that blur boundaries.

Offices populated by women further illustrate the challenges of women's often fluid boundaries with each other. Bosses may feel they cannot be too direct because strong words may hurt feelings that stay hurt for ages and that result in counterproductive behaviors like passive-aggressiveness and gossiping. When listening to women trying to manage a conflict, some men wonder: "Why can't they just talk about what's the matter?" Some women leaders even prefer to work with men, because men tend to keep things simpler and are more susceptible to persuasion (or, as one leader noted, "manipulation").

Before I was aware of these dangers, I fell into the trap of assuming that a professional colleague would remain a friend after our roles shifted. Over time, I discovered that many women experience being undermined or dropped by a woman colleague they'd celebrated as a friend.[105] Certainly, all relationships morph, and friendship can take many forms. But discovering that a friendship you had experienced as reciprocal was not mutual can be deeply painful.

Women unconsciously hold women friends to higher standards of mutuality than they hold men to. This expectation, combined with lack of courage in broaching sensitive topics, contributes to relational failures. And since the playing fields remain steeply tilted in favor of the most ambitious, expecting women to be less competitive than men is a setup for disappointment. For example, when women medical students expect the women surgeons to be "nicer" than the men and their hopes are not met, they usually blame these success-

---

105.   Janet Bickel, "Why Do Women Hamper Other Women?" *Journal of Women's Health* 23 (2014): 365-7.

ful women rather than examine their own gendered assumptions. Fortunately, once women professionals learn to navigate these tricky waters, most establish many enduring friendships that remain functional even as roles shift.

Delays in Becoming the Protagonist

Wearing a green sash with mostly meaningless "merit" badges, I belted out the Girl Scouts' theme song,[106] embodying what girls in the 1950s were supposed to aspire to: sincerity, courtesy, loyalty. In high school, I did not question why I was the only girl in physics class. In college, I didn't notice that not one member of the English department faculty was a woman, or that, despite top grades, I was not considered a candidate for graduate school.

The stories I grew up with reinforced these gender blinders. With marriage as women's substitute for self-determination, women never get to, with Huck, "light out for the Territory."[107] Dorothy in Oz longs to go home—and to what? Marriage with a farmhand? Joseph Campbell's "hero with a thousand faces" are all male, and this trend continues—from Moses to Odysseus to Harry Potter. Linda Austin, a psychiatrist, points out that "women are allowed to be good but not great."[108] An elemental gulf separates an adventurer from an adventuress.

The male gaze—a sexualized point of view that empowers men and objectifies women—still dominates films and other media.

---

106. "She wears a G for generosity. She wears an I for interest, too. She wears an R for real sportsmanship. She wears an L for loyalty, for loyalty! She wears an S for her sincerity. She wears a C for courtesy. She wears an O-U-T for outdoor life, outdoor life. And that Girl Scout is Me!"

107. Bruce Handy, *Wild Things: Reading Children's Literature as an Adult* (Simon & Schuster, 2017).

108. Linda Austin, *What's Holding You Back? Eight Critical Choices for Women's Success* (Basic Books, 2000).

Consider how few serious movies meet even the minimal criteria known as the Bechdel Test: there are at least two named women who talk to each other about something other than a man. That is, the women have their own narrative arc that is not about supporting a man's story. Another result of the male gaze is a great deal of overlap in how women are portrayed in ads and films: tall, slender, big eyes, big mouth. No wonder girls develop body image problems. Spending a fortune on cosmetic surgery, hair removal, and makeup, even mature women remain preoccupied with their appearance.

Women protagonists are beginning to appear—although as author Jia Tolentino noted, the heroines of young adult fiction (for example, Katniss in *The Hunger Games*) are frequently "blind to their own bravery ... forming a crucial part of their appeal to male characters."[109] In other words, women awakened to their own strengths are not biddable enough to remain attractive to any but the most sexually secure men, of whom there has never been a surplus.

Self-Differentiation

When it comes to caring for children and keeping a family together, women put others' needs ahead of their own. But even when women are free to attend to their own needs, the socialization of many to stay attuned to and care for others often reduces the energy available to them to pursue their own goals. Some never outgrow their hesitation to close their door.

For those with many relational commitments, there is always a tension between a focus on themselves and a focus on the needs

---

109. Jia Tolentino, *Trick Mirror: Reflections on Self-Delusion* (Random House, 2019).

of others. Many women live in fear of disappointing someone. I've found it helpful to think of this tension as movement along a spectrum between self-differentiation and attunement. Attunement, which is influenced by hormones, is an emotional sensing of another person. This keying into and attending to others ensures the continuation of the human race by channeling the nurture on which civilization depends.

At the other end of the spectrum is self-differentiation. When we self-differentiate, we remain strongly connected to our own experience and clear about our own beliefs and needs. This is the path to agency and to the power to influence events. Agency requires holding boundaries and developing aspects of ourselves that others near us may not understand or welcome. Agency is the precursor of ambition. Ambitions are both a product of and, eventually, a source of affirmation[110]—and we all need affirmation to keep growing.

Learning to control where we land on the spectrum between self-differentiation and attunement is key to our becoming the protagonist—the main character—in our own lives.

How Do We Measure Progress?

The numbers of women in most professions have greatly increased since 1972 when Title IX prohibited sex-based discrimination in programs receiving federal funding. But numbers of women in a given organization turn out to be much less telling than the quality of leadership selection processes, a working environment based on equity and collaboration, and the availability of parental and child care supports. These are harder to measure.

---

110. Anna Fels, *Necessary Dreams: Ambition in Women's Changing Lives* (Pantheon, 2004).

While women face fewer restrictions now than earlier generations endured, many battles remain current and have never eased up. As an example supplied by journalist Theresa Vargas, women of color who are rising professionals still report a feeling of having more in common with the parking garage attendant than with their white peers. She writes, moreover, that we compound the loneliness of inequities by hiding parts of ourselves and then feeling angry about having to do so.[111] Patricia Lockwood depicts her anger as "radiat[ing] out ... in great bronze spikes, like holiness in old paintings .... I know women are supposed to be strong enough now to strangle patriarchs between their powerful thighs, but most of us are affected by male systems and anger in ways we can't articulate or overcome." Audre Lorde shared what her young daughter said about anger: "If you keep ignoring it, it gets madder ... and if you don't speak it out ... it will just up and punch you in the mouth from the inside."[112]

But when it comes to the freedom to express anger, men have freedom, and women and people of color have almost none.[113] Expressing anger is always "unbecoming" in women. Anna Deavere Smith relates that the "nice" expected during her interviews for college was "a performance left over from slavery and Jim Crow, when not to be nice was a potential death sentence .... [Now] a new generation of sisters who no longer perform 'niceness' have a palpable sense of their vulnerability."[114]

---

111. Theresa Vargas, "Nikole Hannah-Jones hasn't started teaching at Howard yet. But already, she's imparting lessons," *The Washington Post,* July 7, 2021, https://www.washingtonpost.com/local/nikole-hannah-jones-lessons-howard/2021/07/07/98fd0568-df3e-11eb-ae31-6b7c5c34f0d6_story.html.

112. Audre Lorde, *The Selected Works of Audre Lorde,* edited by Roxane Gay (W. W. Norton and Company, 2020).

113. Margo Jefferson, *Negroland: A Memoir* (Pantheon Books, 2015).

114. Anna Deavere Smith, "We Were the Last of the Nice Negro Girls," *The Atlantic,* March 2021, 15-17.

In many organizations, even a highly regarded woman leader is easy to dislodge: reduce her already below-average salary, keep her off key committees, attack or misrepresent her, force her to sign a nondisclosure agreement. She either has to live with massive reductions of her influence, find another job (potentially involving moving her family or living apart from them), or file a sex discrimination lawsuit. I know a number of brilliant women who have endured all of these tortures. Some just disappear from the leadership circuit; others move on and slowly rebuild their influence elsewhere.

Those who feel ethically obligated to support culture change by filing suit do so at great professional and personal cost. Retaliation against the plaintiff usually convinces her to leave, scaring off others from bringing forward any complaints. Deep-pocketed institutions introduce delays that drag on for years, during which plaintiffs cannot discuss their cases with colleagues who remain in the dark about the circumstances. These colleagues may even be deposed and pressured by the employer to take the employer's side. As is usually true for whistleblowers, seeking justice and institutional improvements is excruciating at every level.

The question "What is a useful measure of progress?" remains unanswered. Until recently, most cultural maps (mother, daughter, appearance, politeness, religion, homemaking, needlework) have reinforced gender stereotypes. These days girls see many more diverse models, but it remains easy for women to slip into the service of men. Novelist Shirley Hazzard wrote: "Nothing creates such untruth in you as the wish to please," and girls still try harder than boys to please and to be "good."

"Girls strive to meet culturally defined standards of shape," writes David Deutsch, "and boys to do their utmost to look strong, thus replicating ancient gender-stereotyping memes which are preventing vast ranges of ideas about what sort of life one should lead from crossing the holders' minds .... If [young people's] thoughts wander in the forbidden direction, they feel uneasiness—and they are left disabled in precisely the way that will draw the next generation into the same patterns."[115]

What needs to happen for more girls to start piloting their own boats and for more boys to be proud to be feminists? Enlightened adults can do better to help young people explore alternatives rather than taking the path of least resistance which, anyway, always feels hard enough.

Beyond Gender

Generalizations based on one characteristic can be only partially accurate, perhaps especially with regard to gender because it reveals so very little about anyone. My biracial 25-year-old godson asks penetrating questions about the possibilities of moving beyond his own conceptions of gender and race. He emailed me: "The world we live in today seems to be shaped by the imaginary forces that those long before us came up with and ingrained in everything. I find that for myself it is impossible to imagine a world where gender and race do not exert themselves on my way of being and thinking, as much as I may try."

We are seeing some recovery from historical divisions between men and women's roles and between people with light and dark skin. As socially constructed distortions are challenged and dissipate, we sense more of our commonalities, and the old asymmetries of power hold less appeal. In a *New Yorker* essay, Geoff Dyer once deadpanned, "At this point any reasonable man supports the end of patriarchy." Much work along these lines remains. May this book serve as a resource for those undertaking and persevering in this vital work.

---

115. David Deutsch, *The Beginning of Infinity: Explanations that Transform the World* (Penguin, 2012).

APPENDIX 2

RECOMMENDED READING

Career and Leadership Development

Block, Peter. *The Answer to How is Yes: Acting on What Matters*, 2002.

Block, Peter. *Community: The Structure of Belonging*, 2008.

Gallwey, Timothy. *The Inner Game of Work: Focus, Learning, Pleasure and Mobility in the Workplace*, 2000.

Goldsmith, Marshall. *What Got You Here Won't Get You There*. 2007.

Goldsmith, Marshall. *Mojo: How to Get It, How to Keep It, How to Get It Back if You Lose It*. Hyperion, 2009.

Heifetz, Ronald and Linsky, Marty, et al. *The Practice of Adaptive Leadership: Tools and Tactics for Changing Your Organization and the World*. 2009.

Isaacs, William. *Dialogue and the Art of Thinking Together*. 1999.

Kegan, Robert and Lahey, Lisa. *Immunity to Change: How to Overcome it and Unlock the Potential in Yourself and Your Organization*. 2009.

Quinn, Robert. *Building the Bridge as You Walk on It: A Guide to Leading Change*. 2004.

Scharmer, C. Otto. *Theory U: Open Mind, Open Heart, Open Will—Leading from the Future as It Emerges*. 2007.

Schwarz, Roger, Davidson Anne, Carlson Peg, et al. *The Skilled Facilitator's Fieldbook: Tips, Tools and Tested Methods for Consultants, Facilitators, Managers, Trainers, and Coaches*. 2005.

Stone, Douglas and Heen, Sheila. *Thanks for the Feedback: The Science and Art of Receiving Feedback Well*. 2014.

Personal Development

de Botton, Alain. *The School of Life: An Emotional Education*. 2019.

Bridges, William. *The Way of Transition: Embracing Life's Most Difficult Moments*. 2001.

Dillard, Annie. *For the Time Being*. 1999.

Epstein, Mark. *The Trauma of Everyday Life*. 2014.

Goldsmith, Marshall. *Triggers: Creating Behavior that Lasts, Becoming the Person You Want to Be*. 2015.

Hollis, James. *Why Good People Do Bad Things: Understanding Our Darker Selves*. 2007; *Finding Meaning in the Second Half of Life*. 2005; *What Matters Most: Living a More Considered Life*. 2009.

Lamott, Anne. *Help, Thanks, Wow: The Three Essential Prayers*. 2012; *Traveling Mercies: Some Thoughts on Faith*. 2000; *Almost Everything: Notes on Hope*. 2018.

Palmer, Parker. *A Hidden Wholeness: The Journey Toward an Undivided Life*. 2009.

Plotkin, Bill. *Soulcraft: Crossing into the Mysteries of Nature and Psyche*. 2003.

Rohr, Richard. *Falling Upward: A Spirituality for the Two Halves of Life*. 2011.

Sapolsky, Robert. *Behave: The Biology of Humans at Our Best and Worst*. 2017.

Schein, Edgar H. *Humble Inquiry: The Gentle Art of Asking Instead of Telling*. 2013.

Schulz, Kathryn. *Being Wrong: Adventures in the Margin of Error*. 2010.

Stone, Douglas, Patton, Bruce, and Heen, Sheila. *Difficult Conversations: How to Discuss What Matters Most*. 1999.

Wheatley, Margaret. *Perseverance*. 2010.

Whyte, David. *Crossing the Unknown Sea: Work as a Pilgrimage of Identity*. (2001); *Consolations: The Solace, Nourishment and Underlying Meaning of Everyday Words*. (2016); *The Three Marriages: Reimagining Work, Self and Relationship*. (2009).

Gender-Related

Austin, Linda. *What's Holding You Back? Eight Critical Choices for Women's Success.* 2000.

Bechdel, Alison. *The Secret to Superhuman Strength.* 2021.

Fels, Anna. *Necessary Dreams: Ambition in Women's Changing Lives.* 2004.

Fine, Cordelia. *Delusions of Gender: How Our Minds, Society and Neuroscience Create Difference.* 2010.

Johnson, Allan. *Privilege, Power and Difference.* 2000.

Konner, Martin. *Women After All: Sex, Evolution and the End of Male Supremacy.* 2015.

McElvaine, Robert. *Eve's Seed: Biology, the Sexes and the Course of History.* 2000.

Oluo, Ijeoma. *Mediocre: The Dangerous Legacy of White Male America.* 2021.

Tolentino, Jia. *Trick Mirror: Reflections on Self-Delusion.* 2020.

Wilkerson, Isabel. *Caste: The Origins of Our Discontents.* 2020.

Mindfulness and Self-Compassion

Chödrön, Pema. *The Places that Scare You: A Guide to Fearlessness in Difficult Times.* 2018. (Or any of her work).

Feldman, Christina. *Silence: How to Find Inner Peace in a Busy World.* 2001.

Goldstein, Joseph and Kornfield, Jack. *Seeking the Heart of Wisdom: The Path of Insight Meditation.* 2001.

Hanh, Thich Nhat. *Touching Peace: Practicing the Art of Mindful Living.* 2009. (Or any of his work).

Inchausti, Robert, ed. *Echoing Silence: Thomas Merton on the Vocation of Writing.* 2007.

Salzberg, Sharon. *Lovingkindness: The Revolutionary Art of Happiness.* 2018.

Siegel, Ronald. *The Mindfulness Solution: Everyday Practices for Everyday Problems.* 2009.

Tan, Chade-Meng. *Search inside Yourself.* 2012.

THANKS

This opportunity to thank those who have inspired and supported me has been fueling my work on this project from its hazy beginning four years ago:

—to my beloved mom, Jean Finley Wetzel (1926-), the wellspring of my wealth.

—to my Bill, who has been presenting me with roses since our senior year in high school (1967), boon companion, expert photographer, editor, designer and furnisher of indoor and outdoor beauty, and cheerful provider of so many services allowing me the leisure to read and write and who blessedly also makes me laugh.

—to my sister Linda Shantz, always there for me and for her whole family.

—to Penny Williamson, ScD, whose transformational Courage to Lead program boosted all the relational and self-compassion capacities foundational to my work as a coach and whose enthusiastic faith in me has never dimmed (no her, no me; she would say, no Parker Palmer, no her).

—to Tony Suchman MD and Diane Rawlins, whose Leading Organizations to Health program fostered my trust in what groups and authentic presence can accomplish.

—to Sharon Griswold MD for her cheerleading belief that I am one badass writer and that I must bring this book to fruition.

—for their steadfast encouragement and help from the start: Al Bradford, Dru Delong, Diane Magrane MD, Arnold Rabson MD, Niki Steckler PhD, Martha S. Taylor.

—for their essential help at a crucial point in the evolution of this project: Stephanie Abbuhl MD, Donna Chen MD, Yvonne Covin MD, Luckett Davidson, Stephanie Dukhovny MD, Ridge Frank-White, Deb German MD, Joshua Hanson MD, Adina Kalet MD, Kelly Pavela, Ruth Siegel PhD, Mark Stein, Miriam Shuchman MD, Alexandra Suchman, Linda Stahl, Valerie Weber MD, Dave Witsell MD.

—for their friendship and subtle support of this writing: Joseph Alejandro, Marien Alejandro, Kathy Amberger, Arlene Balkansky, Diane Ballard, Nancy Bennett, Linda Clever MD, Nancy Daly, Liz Donnelly, Ellen Feaver, Marian Fetter, Margaret Gregory, Mary Hale, Sarah Houston, Sue Houston, Karla Jutzi, Joseph Keyes JD, Tom Karl, Peg Kroll, Irina Lajeunesse, Barb Mahony, Renee Marshall, Gayle Monkenon, Patty Phillips, Michelle Pollock, Elaine Porter, Pat Scheel, Trish Stefanik, Nancy Swift, Kim Theodore, Sadie Velásquez MD, Carolyn Whitehead, Mimi Zinniel.

—to generative colleagues for their guiding examples of commitment to excellence and professional service: Lou Andrew MD JD, Shari Barkin MD, Emelia Benjamin MD PhD, Greg Bowling MD, Pam Charney MD, Rita Charon MD, Jordan Cohen MD, Pat Eiff MD, Carola Eisenberg MD, Clyde Evans PhD, Erica Frank MD, Martin Feder PhD, Pierre Galletti MD PhD, Julie Rivera Gilbreath MD, Maureen Goodenough PhD, Larrie Greenberg MD, J.A. Grisso MD, Mary Guerrera MD, Rebecca Harrison MD, Katherine Hartmann MD PhD, Jennifer Havens MD, Sharon Hostler MD, Thomas Innui MD, Anitha Johns MD, Annette Johnson MD, Susan Johnson MD, Ruth Kirschstein MD, Rachel Levine MD, Luci Leykum MD, Mark Linzer MD, Debra Litzelman MD, Ana Maria Lopez MD, Tony Mazzaschi, Carolyn Meltzer MD, Kathryn Montgomery PhD, Page Morahan PhD, Chris Moreland MD, Pete Morris MD, Catherine Morrison PhD, Carol Nadelson MD, Lois Nora MD JD, Jane O'Rorke

MD, Christine Peterson MD, Maureen Phipps MD, Vivian Pinn MD, John-Henry Pfifferling PhD, Gail Povar MD, Ambili Ramachandran MD, Temple Ratcliffe MD, Sally Rosen MD, Kevin Schindler MD, Jen Schlener, Hanna Sherman MD, Kim Skarupski PhD, Eleanor Shore MD, Jeannette South-Paul MD, Emma Stokes PhD, Kat Turner, Amparo Villablanca, MD, Norma Wagoner PhD, Diane Wara MD, Gretchen Wells MD, Janet Williams MD, Wendy Wolf MD.

Finally, thanks to the invaluable help of my Publishing Partner, Bethany Kelly and editor, Olivia Bauer

Made in the USA
Middletown, DE
11 November 2022